CAVEMAN DELEGATION

The Leadership Secret That's Been Around Since the Stone Age

DALLAS BURNETT

Thrive
Publishing, LLC

Copyright © 2025 by Dallas Burnett
First Hardback and Paperback Edition 02-25-001

All rights reserved. No part of this publication may be reproduced, distributed, or transmitted in any form or by any means, including photocopying, recording, or other electronic or mechanical methods, without the prior written permission of the publisher, except in the case of brief quotations embodied in critical reviews and certain other noncommercial uses permitted by copyright law. For permission requests, write to the publisher, addressed "Attention: Permissions Coordinator," at the address or website below.

Thrive Publishing, LLC
141 Traction St
Unit #22
Greenville, SC 29611
www.ThinkMoveThrive.com

Some names, businesses, places, events, locales, incidents, and identifying details inside this book have been changed to protect the privacy of individuals.

Ordering Information:
For details, contact the publisher at the address above.
Orders by U.S. trade bookstores and wholesalers. IngramSpark Distribution: Tel: US and Canada: +1 (855) 99SPARK or (855) 997-7225 United Kingdom: +44 808 164 8277 Australia: +61 3 9765 4800

Publisher's Cataloging-in-Publication data

Burnett, Dallas.

Caveman Delegation: *The Leadership Secret That's Been Around Since the Stone Age* / Dallas Burnett

ISBN 978-1-7325353-6-7 (cloth); ISBN 978-1-7325353-7-4 (paper);
ISBN 978-1-7325353-8-1 (ebk);

BUS041000 BUSINESS & ECONOMICS / Management
BUS071000 BUSINESS & ECONOMICS / Leadership

Printed in the United States of America

Dedicated to my first English teacher—my mom—and my first coach—my dad.

CONTENTS

...

PREFACE:	HOW A CAVEMAN CAME TO LIFE	1
INTRODUCTION:	OF ANTS AND ELEPHANTS	5
CHAPTER 1:	THE ART AND SCIENCE OF DELEGATION	9
CHAPTER 2:	RECOGNIZING WHEN TO DELEGATE	21
CHAPTER 3:	CRAFTING YOUR DELEGATION STRATEGY	35
CHAPTER 4:	THE "WHO" OF DELEGATION	53
CHAPTER 5:	THE "HOW" OF DELEGATION	61
CHAPTER 6:	DELEGATION DESIGNED FOR SUCCESS	73
CHAPTER 7:	OVERCOMING CHALLENGES, NAVIGATING THE OBSTACLES	91
CHAPTER 8:	TEAM AWARENESS WINS THE DAY	101
CHAPTER 9:	HARNESSING YOUR ENNEAGRAM SUPERPOWERS	111
CHAPTER 10:	TAILORING COMMUNICATION AND MOTIVATION	119
CHAPTER 11:	LEADERSHIP DEVELOPMENT AND LEGACY	125
CHAPTER 12:	THE HEART OF LEADERSHIP	131
BIBLIOGRAPHY BY CHAPTER		137
ACKNOWLEDGMENTS		143
RESOURCES		145

PREFACE:
HOW A CAVEMAN CAME TO LIFE

• • •

Are you cursed? What if you are but don't even know it—walking around day and night under an invisible curse? The kind that haunts you, drives you crazy, exhausts you, and makes you question why you even bother getting out of bed. If you were cursed, how would you know? You'd be stressed and grumpy. Never able to see the silver lining, never able to stop and smell the roses, never able to come up for air. You'd be ever-weighted down. Crushed and burdened. Living a life that looks light and fluffy on the outside but harbors a very dark center. If you were cursed, you wouldn't know what to do about it or how to get rid of it. You'd be lost and broken... hopeless.

That was my curse. I realized it one afternoon while riding on a lawn mower, listening to a leadership podcast and thinking something was missing. What curse was I living under? What curse might be plaguing your life too? It was the curse of capability—the curse of "I can, so I should."

Are you a capable person? Do you know how to get things done? Maybe you're a planner, an achiever, an innovator. Capability comes in all shapes and sizes. My capability curse was that I could do lots of things well—better than the average bear. Now you might be wondering, "Is this guy nuts?" Why would being able to get stuff done or having many strengths be a curse? Let me explain.

I was running a venture-funded startup that was growing fast. I was also the father of three daughters—ages 5, 4, and 2. We lived on a small 50-acre farm with chickens, goats, cows, and a dog named Maggie. The American dream, right? Well, maybe, but it didn't feel like it. In fact, I was miserable.

Each morning, I'd rise early to beat traffic on my 50-minute commute, work long hours, and try to grow the business. In the beginning, I was chief cook and bottle washer—handling admin, marketing, support, training, HR, and anything else needed. When our church asked us to lead a small group at our house every Monday night, I thought, "I could, so I should."

My wife was staying home with the kids, so to save money, I bought a nice mower to cut our grass. Doesn't sound so bad, right? Who doesn't love the hum of a mower on a Saturday morning? I could, so I should! But our yard wasn't a half-acre—it was ACRES of grass with trees and fencing that needed not just mowing but weed-eating too. It took 8-10 hours to cut our yard in the country.

And that's just scratching the surface. We haven't even touched on the volunteer work, coaching girls' soccer teams, or leading worship on Sunday morning (plus greeting at the front door before service). Sound like a real achiever? A real trooper? More like someone headed for a mental breakdown.

I was busy but not happy. Productive-ish but not thriving. What was I? Tired. The breaking point came when we bought an Airbnb next to our property. My wife picked paint colors, decorated the whole house, and booked our first guests. She decided we didn't need a property manager or cleaner because "she could, so she should!" The week before guests arrived, our builder—who was supposed to help finish some remodeling—completely bailed on us with just five days' notice. I spent Labor Day weekend laying flooring for 14 hours a day just to have enough time to clean and furnish the last room before check-in.

No days off. No downtime. No breaks. So there I was, the next Saturday on my mower, listening to a leadership podcast (because that's what "could-and-shoulders" do when they cut grass). The topic was delegation. The guest had his method of describing it, and I thought, "That's great, but no one will ever remember how to do that when it counts." Then it hit me: "I am HORRIBLE at delegation, and that might be why I'm so miserable!"

When we don't have boundaries, when we're very capable, when we're pleasers—or all three—we tend to take things in but never give them up. If we're being honest with ourselves (as I had to be on that mower), we're lazy and scared.

It seems impossible to use the "L" word when describing such achievements. But it's true, and that's why the curse maintains its power. I didn't want to do the real work of finding someone to cut my grass. I made excuses: they wouldn't do it as well as me, it would be too expensive. Why pay a cleaner for the Airbnb when we could handle it in our "free time?"

What if no one could lead a small group like us? What if we needed to rotate less on the worship team? What if I needed to hire an executive assistant or more team members, and they weren't capable? What if I needed to get rid of the chickens? For capable people, it's easier to continue doing energy-draining tasks than to confront the idea of letting go.

Part of my curse was feeling I "should" be able to do all these things, and if I couldn't (while being a great dad), I was a failure. What a curse. When I stepped back, I realized I wasn't living up to my potential in almost any area of my life. I took shortcuts on the yard because I had to start at 5 AM to cut some before work so I could coach soccer on weekends. I was never prepared for practice because I came straight from work. I couldn't find 20 minutes each night to practice music for Sunday worship. I was living my worst nightmare—unable to keep up with the "shoulds."

That's why I'm writing this book. That Saturday afternoon on the lawn mower, I became keenly aware of my need to say "no" and delegate better. It hit me like a bolt of lightning. My new delegation system was so easy even... well, you can finish the GEICO commercial. The Caveman Delegation System was born, and I started implementing it the next week.

Over the years, I've honed these ideas and become a much better delegator. Today, I'm more productive than ever before. I'm better at the activities that truly matter, and I'm a better husband and father. It's been years since I spent 8 hours cutting grass. We have an amazing cleaner for the Airbnb. I hired dozens of employees at the startup, and even after I transitioned out, it kept growing and recently sold for tens of millions of dollars. One of my early hires even became COO.

I believe in the importance of delegation. We need great leaders—not burnt-out leaders who are miserable. I hope the ideas and simple system outlined in this book help you take your delegation skills to the next level. If it seems overwhelming, just start by writing down one thing you can try to hand off when you finish reading this book. Happy reading!

INTRODUCTION:
OF ANTS AND ELEPHANTS

• • •

In organizations and teams, there are big initiatives and vision statements. These are an organization's "elephants"—they're large, commanding, and you don't want to mess with their tusks, or you might get trampled! It's crucial that we align our actions and intentions with these elephants and our company's values.

For most people, this isn't a complicated idea. When organizations are clear on their mission, vision, and values—and intentional about creating a culture around them—they naturally promote people who align with these ideas. If you're a leader reading this book on delegation, you're well aware of your organization's elephants.

However, there's another creature lurking in every organization. One that's often overlooked and misjudged but can be more dangerous to a leader because of its unassuming nature: ants. There's a South African proverb that says, "Even an ant can hurt an elephant." This simple wisdom reminds us that even the smallest, seemingly insignificant things can have a powerful impact.

So what are the ants in our organizations? They're the small things that slowly sap your energy, take away your strength, and drain your life while relentlessly pursuing your time. Ants are those minor tasks you're not particularly skilled at completing. They're team members who rely on you to finish their work. They're the piles of emails in your inbox. They're the things you know you need to address but keep shoving to the back of your mind. All these tiny ants are slowly but surely attacking your spirit.

The danger of ants shouldn't be underestimated. In 1903, a tragic story emerged from Australia. Michael Harold lived alone in a hut on the Thurgoona property of Mr. and Mrs. Day. After noticing his absence, the Days searched for him, only to find Mr. Harold lying unconscious in his hut, covered in ants that were eating into his body. The ants had entered his ears, nostrils, and mouth. He never regained consciousness and died in Albury Hospital later that week. This horrible tragedy illustrates why the South African proverb rings so true: DON'T UNDERESTIMATE ANTS!

Does this sound familiar? You're juggling a dozen tasks, your inbox is overflowing, and your to-do list seems to grow longer by the minute. If you're nodding your head, you're not alone. Welcome to the world of leadership, where the weight of responsibility often feels like a heavy backpack you can never unload. But beware—these urgent items can either distract you from the elephants or literally suck the life right out of you.

We need to lighten that load. To fight the ants! We need a way to accomplish more, empower our teams, and reclaim our time while staying focused on the elephants. That's where delegation comes in—the secret weapon of successful leaders.

Delegation isn't just about assigning tasks. It's an art form, a delicate dance of trust, communication, and strategy. It's about recognizing the potential in others and giving them the opportunity to shine. It's about focusing your energy where it matters most and enabling your team to grow alongside you.

But let's be honest—delegation isn't always easy. Many leaders struggle with knowing when and what to delegate. You might have thought, "It'll be quicker if I just do it myself," or "No one else can do it quite like I can." These thoughts are common, but they hold you back from becoming the most effective leader you can be.

In this book, we'll explore the ins and outs of effective delegation. We'll debunk common myths, tackle the fears that hold leaders back, and provide practical strategies to help you become a delegation pro. From knowing when and what to delegate to choosing the right person for the job, we'll cover it all.

You'll learn about innovative approaches like the Caveman Delegation Method, which offers a step-by-step guide to transferring responsibilities effectively. We'll also dive into real-world examples—both successes and cautionary tales—to illustrate the power of delegation done right.

Whether you're a seasoned executive looking to fine-tune your skills or a new manager taking your first steps into leadership, this book is for you. By the time you finish reading, you'll have the tools and confidence to transform your leadership style and your team's performance through the art of delegation.

As we journey together, you'll learn not only how to delegate but how to build a culture of accountability and trust within your team. Whether you're leading a small group or an entire organization, mastering delegation will elevate your leadership and help your team achieve more.

So, are you ready to let go of the reins a little and watch your team soar? Let's embark on this journey together and unlock the full potential of delegation in your leadership toolkit.

CHAPTER 1:
THE ART AND SCIENCE OF DELEGATION

■ ■ ■

> "Don't tell people how to do things, tell them what to do and let them surprise you with their results."
> **- George S. Patton**

The Art of Being a Conductor

Imagine you're conducting an orchestra. As the conductor, your job isn't to play every instrument – it's to bring out the best in each musician, creating harmony from individual talents. That's what great delegation looks like in action.

Delegation is more than just a management technique; it's a fundamental leadership skill that can make or break your success. At its core, delegation is the act of entrusting tasks or responsibilities to others. But it's more than just passing the buck. Effective delegation is about empowering your team, maximizing efficiency, and focusing your energy where it's needed most.

When we conduct an orchestra, it's clear that no single leader can play every instrument. Similarly, delegation is an essential strategy for unlocking a team's potential and achieving success within an organization. According to research, effective delegation can boost efficiency and improve employee performance(Leana, 1986). By sharing responsibilities, leaders allow team members to grow, acquire new skills, and make valuable contributions to common goals. This blend of teamwork and personal development is what turns delegation from a simple task into a transformative leadership practice.

The Psychology Behind Effective Delegation
Why do some leaders struggle with delegation while others seem to do it effortlessly? It often comes down to psychology. Many of us have an innate desire for control, a fear of failure, or a belief that "if you want something done right, you have to do it yourself." These mindsets can be major roadblocks to effective delegation

But here's the truth: **letting go doesn't mean losing control**. In fact, it often leads to better outcomes. When you delegate effectively, you're tapping into the diverse skills and perspectives of your team. You're creating opportunities for growth and innovation that simply can't happen when you try to do everything yourself.

> The best delegators see the potential in people, not just the tasks at hand.

Delegation is not about shirking responsibilities or avoiding work; it's about <u>focusing on the responsibilities that truly require your attention and expertise</u> while empowering your team to take ownership of other tasks. This is where great leaders excel—they understand that leadership isn't about doing everything themselves but about maximizing the potential of their teams. John Maxwell, in *The 21 Irrefutable Laws of Leadership*, emphasizes that delegation is a key way to empower others, increase your own effectiveness, and drive results. Take it from John Maxwell: As a delegator and leader, you can spend more time on the most important, strategic activities and activities that naturally give you energy.

Debunking Delegation Myths

Despite the many benefits of delegation, many leaders hesitate to fully embrace it. This hesitation is often rooted in common fears or misconceptions about delegation. Let's address some of the most common myths and barriers that hold leaders back.

Myth 1:
"I Can Do It Faster Myself"

This is one of the most common reasons leaders hesitate to delegate. While it's true that doing a task yourself might be faster in the short term, it's not a sustainable approach. **Delegation is an investment in the long-term growth of your team.** It may take time to teach someone how to do a task, but once they've mastered it, you'll save that time many times over. According to a study published by Havard Business Review, effective delegation can save leaders up to 20% of their time in the long run.

By holding onto tasks because "it's faster to do it myself," you're not only limiting your own effectiveness but also preventing your team from growing into their full potential. A study published in the *Academy of Management Journal* highlights that **delegation positively affects job satisfaction and team member performance.**

Myth 2:
"Delegation is a Sign of Weakness"

Some leaders believe that delegating tasks will make them appear less capable or less in control. However, the opposite is true—delegation is a sign of strong leadership. It shows that **you trust your team** and are focused on the bigger picture.

Delegation isn't a sign of weakness; it's a sign of wisdom.

Strong leaders understand that their success is tied to the success of their team, and delegation is one of the most effective ways to empower others and multiply your impact.

Myth 3:
"What if They Mess Up?"

The fear of mistakes often prevents leaders from delegating. But mistakes are a natural part of the learning process. When you delegate tasks, there may be a learning curve, and that's okay. The key is to provide the necessary support, guidance, and feedback to help your team learn from those mistakes and improve over time.

As we'll discuss later in the book, delegation is a gradual process, and frameworks like the **Caveman Delegation Method** can help ensure that tasks are delegated in a way that reduces the risk of mistakes while building confidence.

The Science of Successful Delegation

Holding on to myths about delegation can be harmful to both ourselves and our teams. Insights from the 2018 Work and

Well-Being Survey conducted by the American Psychological Association show that nearly one-third of U.S. workers reported that their workload makes it difficult to take time off. Additionally, around one in five workers avoid taking time off due to feelings of guilt, fearing that it may be perceived as a lack of commitment to their job. However, there is hope when leaders learn to let go of these myths and delegate effectively. According to a Gallup survey, **CEOs with strong delegation skills generated 33% more revenue in 2013.** So, it is possible to find success and, at the same time, take vacations guilt-free.

So, what makes delegation successful? It's about matching the right tasks with the right people at the right time. This is where methods like the Caveman Delegation Method come into play, providing a structured approach to gradually transfer responsibilities. Before we dive into the Caveman Delegation Method, it's essential to discuss a few tools to ensure we get it right. One of the most critical aspects of successful delegation and coaching is clarity.

Clarity: The Foundation for Effective Delegation

In 2018, I wrote the book ***MOVE!*** and devoted significant time to the concept of clarity In both our personal and professional lives, we benefit from clarity and actively seek it. Clarity involves moving from the general to the specific; it is about perceiving reality in a coherent manner. Delegation also begins with clarity. Without it, even the most well-intentioned delegation efforts can result in miscommunication, inefficiency, and frustration for both leaders and their teams. Clarity isn't just about knowing what needs to be done—it's about illuminating the purpose, narrowing the focus, and framing the task or responsibility. These three elements—**light, focus, and frame**—serve as a powerful foundation for making intentional delegation decisions.

Light

Imagine walking into a dark room and being asked to find a single book on a shelf. Without light, the task feels impossible. Similarly, without purpose, delegation lacks direction. The first step in effective delegation is to shed light on the "why" behind the task.

Every task or responsibility exists for a reason. Leaders often assume the purpose is obvious, but team members may not share the same context. By clearly explaining why a task matters and how it aligns with broader organizational goals, leaders not only create a sense of meaning but also empower their teams to approach the work with greater commitment. Light is the "big idea" that sets the stage for all the action that follows.

Example: A project manager assigns the creation of a monthly report to a team member without explaining its purpose. The report ends up being a box-checking exercise, adding little value. If the manager had illuminated the purpose—such as helping the leadership team make data-driven decisions to outperform the competition—the team member might have approached the task with more thoughtfulness and creativity.

When you shine a light on the purpose, you transform delegation from a simple transaction into an opportunity for alignment and impact.

Focus

Everyone has taken a blurry picture on their phone or camera. When you adjust your lens, you start to see clear details—where one object ends and another begins and the depth of the scene. The same principle applies to delegation. Leaders must identify which aspects of a task or responsibility require their unique skills and which can be entrusted to others. This requires an honest assessment of your strengths and the strengths of your team.

Without focus, leaders can fall into the trap of spreading their attention too thin or focusing on the wrong things and micromanaging every detail. Delegation thrives when leaders concentrate on the high-impact areas where they add the most value, leaving other aspects to capable team members.

Example: A sales leader struggling to manage client relationships and team performance decides to focus on nurturing top accounts while delegating administrative tasks like CRM updates and scheduling to an assistant. By narrowing their attention, the leader improves client retention and boosts team morale.

Focus not only prevents burnout but also ensures that leaders and their teams are working on the right things. When you delegate well, you increase your focus while helping others develop.

Frame

Even with light and focus, delegation can struggle without the right context. Have you ever visited an amusement park with a room designed to resemble an old Wild West saloon? You can dress up in period clothing with your family, and when the picture is taken, it develops without vibrant colors, resulting in a grey or brown appearance reminiscent of photographs from the 1800s. The context we provide enhances our picture by adding color or taking it away.

Framing is about defining where the task starts and finishes and adding context—what success looks like, what resources are available, and what boundaries exist.

Leaders often hesitate to delegate because they fear losing control. However, a well-framed task gives both the leader and the team member confidence. It provides the structure needed for autonomy while ensuring accountability.

Example: A department head asks a team member to draft a presentation for an upcoming client meeting but fails to set expectations about the tone, key messages, or time allocation. The resulting presentation misses the mark. If the leader had framed the task by outlining its objectives and providing a sample template, the team members could have delivered a more targeted result.

Framing creates a shared understanding, enabling delegation to move forward smoothly. Now, we can look at a tool that was also covered in ***MOVE!*** and can help provide clarity on delegation.

Applying the Mindful Quadrant to Delegation

The Mindful Quadrant provides a deeper layer of insight into how leaders can approach delegation with intention. It asks four transformative questions: **What do I harbor? What do I lack? What do I cultivate? What do I starve?** Each question serves as a lens for understanding your delegation habits and priorities. We can add them to the quadrant below and will discuss each one in detail.

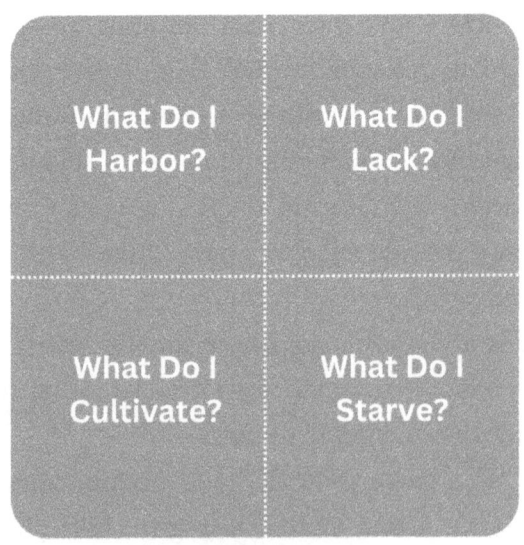

The Mindful Quadrant
Source: MOVE!

What Do I Harbor?

Harboring refers to the things leaders protect or cling to, often unconsciously. Think of a harbor for boats or ships. It's a place of protection from the dangers of the open sea. While some harboring is positive—such as protecting high-value activities—other forms can hinder delegation. For instance, leaders might harbor a fear of losing control, perfectionism, or emotional attachment to tasks that no longer serve their role.

> Evaluate what you're harboring. Are you holding onto tasks out of habit or fear? Conversely, what should you intentionally protect to delegate effectively? For example, a leader might harbor a sense of ownership over client relationships but delegate the administrative side of account management to maintain focus on strategy.

What Do I Lack?

When we lack something, we are keenly aware of its absence. We can lack personal connections, money in our budget, project resources, or even time with our team members. Lacking clarity, trust, or systems can create roadblocks to delegation. Leaders might hesitate to delegate because they feel their team isn't ready or because processes aren't in place to ensure success. Delegation can also reveal gaps in team capacity or resources.

> Identify what's missing. If you lack trust, invest in training and communication to build confidence. If you lack systems, create clear SOPs to streamline delegation. By addressing these gaps, you pave the way for more effective delegation.

What Do I Cultivate?

When we think of the word "cultivation," what comes to mind? One simple example is the act of planting, watering, and growing a garden. Cultivation is about routinely nurturing the conditions needed to produce success. Regarding delegation, this includes building trust, fostering team autonomy, and developing skills. Leaders who cultivate growth in their team members empower them to take on more responsibility.

> Ask yourself what you need to cultivate within your team and your organization to delegate more effectively. This could mean mentoring team members, creating opportunities for skill-building, or fostering a culture of accountability.

What Do I Starve?

Sometimes, there are areas in our work and life where we need to starve. As we look at what steals our time or energy during the day, some activities are unnecessary. When we starve something, we remove its ability to thrive. We intentionally want to see it wither because it is not helping produce our desired result. To create space for effective delegation, leaders must starve the habits, mindsets, or processes that no longer serve them. This might include perfectionism, micromanagement, or overcommitment.

> Consider what you need to let go of to make delegation work. For instance, a leader who micromanages might need to starve the habit of constantly checking in and instead focus on setting clear expectations upfront.

Bringing Clarity to the Delegation Line

With the insights from the clarity framework and the Mindful Quadrant, you are more equipped to begin the work of delegation. By examining what you harbor, lack, cultivate, and starve, you can address the deeper dynamics that influence your delegation decisions.

Example: A CEO reviewing their task list might realize they're harboring a fear of delegating operational oversight despite having a capable COO. By applying the Mindful Quadrant, they decide to cultivate trust through regular check-ins and starve the habit of double-checking every report, allowing the COO to take full ownership.

As you move forward, consider how these tools can help you approach delegation with greater confidence and intentionality. What will you illuminate, focus on, frame, harbor, lack, cultivate, or starve? The answers to these questions will define your leadership legacy.

Embracing the Art of Letting Go

Wow! We are just getting started in our journey to becoming "Delegation Jedis." Delegation is as much an art as it is a science. It requires empathy, communication skills, and a keen understanding of your team's strengths and weaknesses. It's about finding the balance between providing support and giving autonomy.

As we move forward in this book, we'll explore practical strategies to help you master this delicate balance. We'll look at when to delegate, what to delegate, and how to do it effectively. We'll also address the fears and challenges that often hold leaders back from delegating.

Don't feel overwhelmed; becoming a great delegator doesn't happen overnight. It's a skill that you'll develop and refine over time. But with practice and the right mindset, you can transform your leadership style and unleash the full potential of your team.

> **True delegation isn't about lightening your load—it's about strengthening your team.**

In the next chapter, we'll dive into recognizing the right moments for delegation – because timing, as they say, is everything.

CHAPTER 2:
RECOGNIZING WHEN TO DELEGATE

...

"As soon as you can afford to delegate what you don't like to do, do it. If somebody can do something 80 percent as good as you think you would have done it yourself, then you've got to let it go."
- Sara Blakely – Founder and CEO of Spanx

The Art of Timing in Delegation

Have you ever watched a skilled surfer catch a wave? They don't paddle frantically at every swell. Instead, they wait patiently, reading the water, feeling the rhythm of the ocean. Then, at just the right moment, they make their move.

Delegation works in much the same way. It's not about offloading tasks at every opportunity. It's about recognizing the perfect moments – those situations where delegation will have the most impact on you, your team, and your organization.

Evidence supports this idea. Studies reveal that successful delegation depends on understanding when and how to involve others in decision-making processes (Yukl & Fu, 1999). Factors like task complexity, team capacity, and organizational goals are important for leaders to weigh when determining the right moments to delegate responsibilities.

Signs That You Need to Delegate

So, when should you delegate? One clear sign is when your to-do list never seems to shrink, no matter how hard you work. If you're spending too much time on tasks that others could handle, that's a signal it might be time to start delegating. When you're capable of doing everything but excelling at nothing, it's time to delegate.

> Your capabilities will only take you as far as your ability to prioritize what matters most.

Here is a list of signs that may mean you need to rethink your work and delegate:

1. **You're feeling overwhelmed**: Your workload is too heavy, and it's preventing you from focusing on high-level responsibilities.
2. **Tasks don't align with your core role**: If you're handling duties that don't require your specific expertise or leadership position, it's a perfect opportunity to delegate.
3. **Your team has the potential to grow**: Delegation is a powerful tool for developing the skills of your team members.
4. **Your to-do list never seems to shrink:** If you're constantly playing catch-up and never making headway, it's time to share the load.
5. **You're working longer hours but accomplishing less:** When you find yourself staying late at the office but not seeing results, delegation can help restore balance.

6. **You're missing deadlines or important details:** Dropping balls is a clear indicator that you've got too much on your plate.
7. **You're feeling stressed and irritable:** If work is affecting your mood and well-being, it's time to reassess your workload.
8. **Your focus is on minor tasks instead of strategy**: If you find yourself stuck in the minutiae, handling details that others could take care of, you're not fulfilling your role as a leader.
9. **You're sacrificing personal time or well-being**: Burnout is real. If work is infringing on your personal life and you're consistently working late or on weekends, it's time to reassess and delegate more effectively.

To illustrate the power of delegation, leadership expert Ken Blanchard, author of *The One Minute Manager*, emphasizes that leaders should delegate tasks whenever they can develop someone else's capabilities while staying focused on what only they can do. It's about creating opportunities for others while ensuring you have the bandwidth to focus on your most valuable responsibilities.

> The greatest leaders don't carry the weight alone; they teach others how to lift.

Organizing Your Activities

As a leader, your success and efficiency rely not only on what you do but also on how you allocate your time. A key to mastering delegation is understanding the concept of the *delegation line*, which separates activities you handle personally from those you entrust to others. Ideally, you want to keep only your highest-value activities above this line—the tasks that align with your skills, strengths, and responsibilities—and delegate the rest. First, we will cover the activity times, and then we will cover how leaders manage this line in different ways, reflecting various approaches to time management and delegation.

In this section, we'll explore four common types of activities that make up a leader's time and the different delegation profiles leaders adopt. Each profile provides a framework to help you evaluate your own habits and identify strategies for a more balanced, efficient workload.

Four Activity Types

In the graphics below, you'll see four categories of activities leaders spend their time on:

1. **High Skill / High Passion**: Activities where you're uniquely gifted and passionate. These tasks energize you and are performed with excellence.
2. **High Skill / Low Passion**: Activities that you're skilled at but don't particularly enjoy. These may not drain you, but they don't provide energy or fulfillment.
3. **Low Skill / High Passion** (Fan-zone): Tasks you enjoy but aren't highly skilled at. While these energize you, they may take longer to complete or lack the quality needed.
4. **Low Skill / Low Passion** (BAD): Activities where you lack both skill and passion. These tasks drain energy, often leaving you grumpy and tired when completed.

Let's apply these four types of activities using the following graphs.

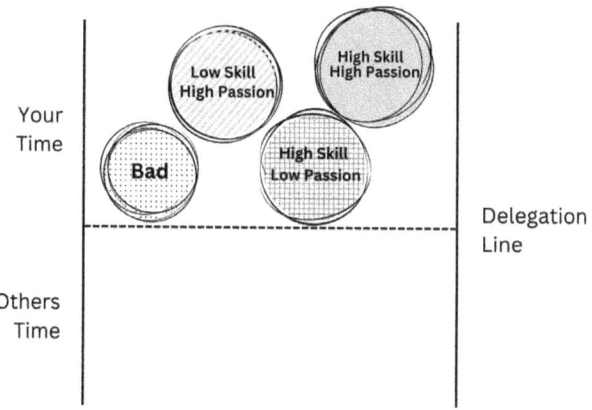

Stressed Leader Time Profile

1. High-Control, High-Stress Approach

This first approach, called the *High-Control, High-Stress* profile, is marked by a leader keeping most tasks above the *delegation line*. They take responsibility for many activities themselves—even those that might be better suited for delegation. This type of leader often says, "If you want it done right, you have to do it yourself."

While this approach might seem efficient for leaders who enjoy being involved in every detail, it quickly leads to burnout and decreased productivity. When you hold on to tasks that don't align with your unique strengths or interests, you end up spending valuable time on activities that drain your energy and create stress. No one can excel at everything, and leaders with a high-control approach often find it difficult to delegate, leading to lower efficiency and a greater risk of burnout.

This approach is unsustainable, as it creates a high-stress environment that limits both personal and team growth. If you recognize this pattern in your own time management style, consider adjusting your delegation strategy to relieve stress and enhance productivity.

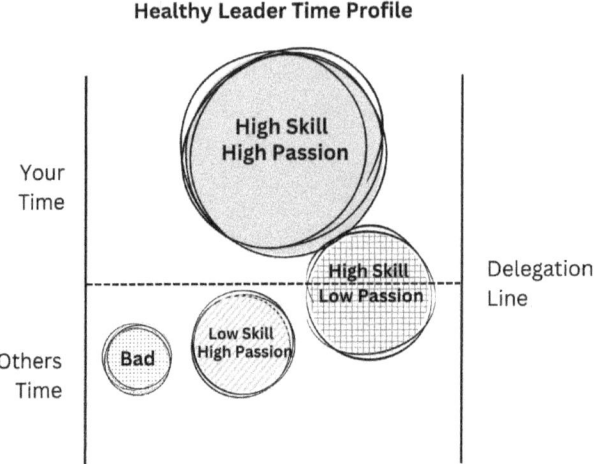

2. Healthy Delegation Approach

The second approach is the *Healthy Delegation* approach, a balanced style of time management. Leaders who follow this approach actively evaluate tasks and strive to keep only those they excel at or find motivating above the delegation line, delegating the rest to team members whose skills align with the tasks.

Leaders practicing intentional delegation recognize that effective leadership involves focusing on high-impact activities that match their strengths. They are comfortable letting go of tasks they aren't particularly skilled at, aren't passionate about, or aren't directly accountable for. This approach not only reduces personal workload and stress but also empowers team members to take ownership and grow in their roles.

It's common for some activities in the *High Skill / Low Passion* category to remain with the leader. This is still considered healthy because these tasks may require specific expertise, access to data, or authority that's not easily transferable. As long as these low-passion tasks take up a small portion of the leader's time, they will still be effective and engaged in their work.

By intentionally delegating tasks outside their core strengths, leaders create an environment where they can operate at their highest capacity, channeling energy into areas where they can make the greatest impact.

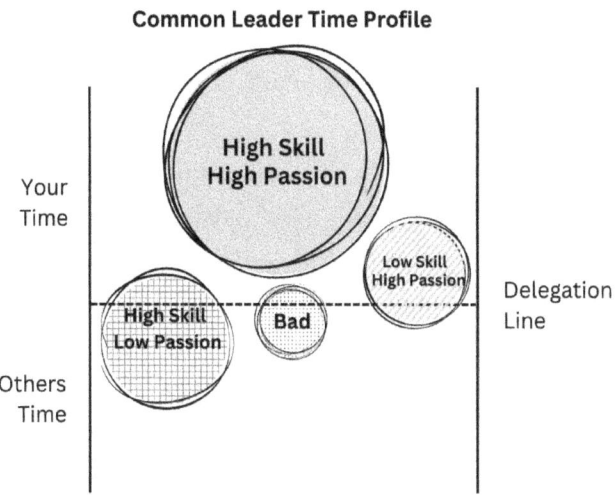

3. Common Delegation Approach

The *Common Delegation* approach reflects a pattern many leaders—especially business owners—fall into. In this profile, the leader has delegated a majority of activities they lack passion for but has kept most activities they enjoy, **even if they aren't highly skilled at them**.

This is the leader who tells everyone they're a fantastic graphic designer and even built the company website. While they enjoyed doing it, the website may be subpar or take months to complete instead of weeks. This is the *Fan Zone*—tasks you enjoy but may not have the skill to complete at a professional level.

For leaders in the Fan Zone, it's helpful to "be a fan" by following the progress and staying updated rather than handling the work directly. This allows you to remain connected to the task without taking on the full workload.

The issue with this delegation approach is that it can prevent the team from reaching its full potential. High performers on the team may become frustrated with the leader's lower quality or slower completion time on certain tasks. Over time, this frustration can grow—or, even worse, the team may begin to accept lower performance as the standard.

Delegation should be approached as a flexible process. Leaders in the Common profile should strive to delegate even the tasks they enjoy but lack the skill to complete at the highest standard, moving closer to an ideal delegation balance.

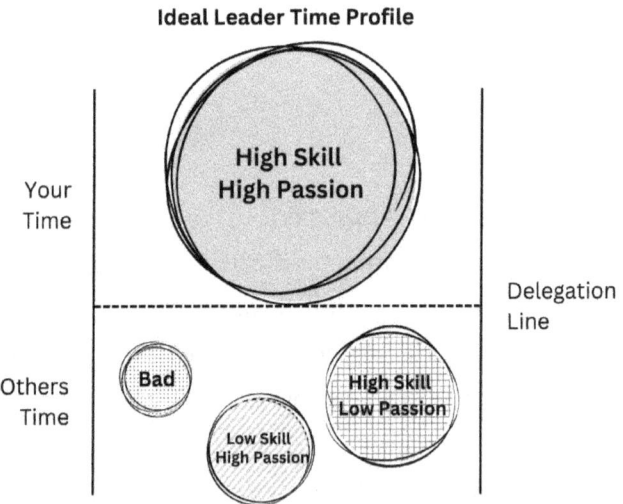

5. Ideal Delegation Approach

The final profile is the Ideal Delegation approach, representing the ultimate goal for most leaders. In this model, the only tasks remaining above the delegation line are those that perfectly align with the leader's unique abilities—tasks where they are both highly skilled and deeply passionate. This ideal state enables leaders to operate at peak efficiency, focusing exclusively on activities that maximize their impact.

However, while this is a valuable target, it's not always achievable. Some responsibilities may be non-negotiable, even if they don't perfectly match a leader's unique strengths. Similarly, limited resources or team capacity might mean certain tasks simply can't be delegated.

Achieving the ideal is a worthwhile pursuit, but leaders should be realistic, aiming to move as close as possible to the ideal state. Rather than dismissing this as unattainable, consider what you can currently delegate to move closer to the ideal. Every small step counts.

Leveraging Your Strengths

The idea of focusing on one's strengths and passions isn't new. Dan Sullivan's concept of *unique abilities*, introduced in his early 2000s book on strengths-based leadership, emphasizes the value of operating within your unique skill set. According to Sullivan, each person has specific abilities they excel at, enjoy, and find naturally fulfilling. When leaders focus on activities that tap into these unique abilities, they work more effectively and experience greater job satisfaction.

In practical terms, identifying your unique abilities allows you to focus your time and energy on tasks that truly matter. Delegating tasks outside of this zone doesn't just lighten your workload— it ensures that you're dedicating yourself to the highest-value activities, the ones where you're most skilled and passionate. Leveraging your unique abilities is essential for a sustainable, productive, and fulfilling work life.

A Practical Rule of Thumb

Many leaders wait until they're overwhelmed to start delegating, but the best leaders practice proactive delegation. Instead of waiting to burn out or be less productive, they actively look for opportunities to delegate tasks that fit their team's strengths and development goals.

One useful guideline for delegation is Jim Schleckser's "70% rule." Jim, the author of "Great CEOs Are Lazy, suggests that:

> If someone can perform a task at least 70% as well as you can, it's time to delegate it.

Holding on to tasks just because you think you can do them slightly better can prevent you from focusing on higher-level responsibilities.

Let's consider an example: Imagine you're responsible for preparing a monthly financial report. It's something you're very good at, but it's also time-consuming. If a team member can handle completing at least 70% of the report without your help, that's an opportunity to delegate. Over time, with feedback and guidance, that team member will likely improve, freeing you up to focus on tasks that are more critical to your role.

It's important to clarify that when we say "70% as good," we are not suggesting that the quality of your work should fall below the required standard of excellence. Everyone needs some time to adapt to a new task in order to gain the experience necessary for improving their performance. Initially, we may need to provide support, training, or extra effort until they can bridge the gap. This is precisely the purpose of the Caveman Delegation Method.

What about an example closer to home? I mentioned during the time I developed the Cavemen Delegation Method, we bought a house that we turned into an Airbnb. Should we try to clean the house in our spare time? That is a great question, but a better question is, could we hire a cleaner that would do at least 70% as good of a job cleaning (on her first day) as us? It's no surprise that we have a fantastic cleaner who enjoys the work and does a great job. Move one more task over the delegation line!

It's important not to get so caught up in the number. You may have noticed at the beginning of the chapter, Sara Blakely said 80%. Other leadership experts like John Maxwell have also echoed 80% instead of 70%. Relax; there is not a tear in the fabric of leadership reality! The point is not the percentage. This concept helps leaders understand they have to **TRUST** others to handle tasks even if they're not perfect from the start. In The 7 Habits of Highly Effective People, Stephen Covey notes that great leaders understand when to let go and allow their team to learn through experience. Delegation becomes an investment in the future, both for your team and for yourself.

Case Study: Effective Delegation in Action

When NASA set out to achieve the seemingly impossible goal of landing a man on the moon, its administrator, James Webb, faced a challenge of astronomical proportions. Webb himself admitted to doubting whether he was the right man for the job. Yet, his leadership style—rooted in intentional and effective delegation—was instrumental in the success of the Apollo program.

Webb recognized early on that managing the immense complexity of the Apollo missions was far beyond the capacity of any single leader. The program demanded expertise across numerous fields, from rocket science to material engineering, requiring not just technical knowledge but also the ability to collaborate under immense pressure. Webb's genius lay in his ability to delegate wisely, empowering a diverse array of experts to take ownership of their respective domains.

One of Webb's key strategies was setting clear expectations while fostering an environment of trust. He provided his team with a compelling vision: achieve President John F. Kennedy's ambitious goal of landing a man on the moon and returning him safely to Earth. Once this vision was established, Webb stepped back, giving his team the authority and autonomy to innovate and make decisions. His leadership style exemplified what delegation should look like: empowering others while maintaining accountability for the mission's overall success.

Webb's delegation wasn't just about handing off tasks; it was about trust. He knew when to intervene and when to let his team members exercise their judgment. By relying on experts like Wernher von Braun for rocket engineering and Gene Kranz for mission operations, Webb ensured that the best minds were in charge of their respective areas. This division of responsibility allowed NASA to solve complex problems, meet tight deadlines, and overcome setbacks without bottlenecks.

The results of Webb's approach were nothing short of historic. On July 20, 1969, the Apollo 11 mission landed Neil Armstrong and Buzz Aldrin on the moon, achieving one of humanity's greatest milestones. Webb's ability to delegate effectively not only ensured the mission's success but also demonstrated how empowering others to lead in their areas of strength can achieve extraordinary outcomes.

Webb's story highlights a timeless truth about delegation: it's not about relinquishing control but about multiplying capability. By trusting his team and delegating intentionally, Webb created a culture where innovation and accountability thrived, proving that great leaders don't just lead—they elevate everyone around them.

In this chapter, we discussed the importance of knowing when to delegate and the signs that indicate it's time to do so. We examined how to review the activities or tasks you perform daily, weekly, or monthly to identify those you are skilled at and passionate about. If you can find someone capable of handling at least 70% of the task as good as you, delegate as much as possible.

In the next chapter, we will focus on crafting a delegation strategy. We will explore how to determine what tasks you should keep and which ones you can let go. Remember, delegating should not be about offloading tasks onto team members only to make your life easier; we refer to that as "**Delegation Bombs**." We will talk more in Chapter 6 about how the "bombs" approach often results in confusion and stress for those involved. But first, let's start crafting our delegation strategy.

CHAPTER 3:
CRAFTING YOUR DELEGATION STRATEGY

■ ■ ■

> "Deciding what not to do is as important as deciding what to do."
> - Steve Jobs

The Art of Choosing What to Let Go

When you're packing for a long trip, you can't take everything with you – you need to choose what's essential and what can be left behind. In the last chapters, we have covered the general idea of delegation and how to recognize when it is time to delegate. Now, if you looked at the delegation time graphs in the last chapter and felt like your profile matched the High-Control, High-Stress Approach, this chapter is for you.

Even after we realize it's time to clear our plates, we still have to decide the most important activities to delegate. But how do we make these decisions? How do we determine what to keep and what to delegate? That's what we'll explore in this chapter.

The challenge is that not all tasks are created equal when it comes to delegation. Some responsibilities are vital to your leadership role, while others can—and should—be handed off.

> Many times, what you let go of is just as important as what you hold on to.

The key to effective delegation is being able to differentiate between these tasks.

Leadership expert Ken Blanchard has consistently emphasized that **leaders who effectively choose what to let go are the ones who drive both personal and team success**. If you are growing a business or growing a team, pay careful attention to this chapter! Let's explore how you can craft your delegation strategy.

Tasks Ready for Delegation

So, how do we decipher what we should delegate? While it may feel uncomfortable at first, many tasks can and should be shared with our team. Here's a breakdown of work typically suitable for delegation:

1. **Repetitive or Routine Tasks:** Tasks that follow a predictable process are ideal for delegation. These might include preparing reports, scheduling meetings, or organizing documents. Once a team member has been trained on the process, they can take ownership of these tasks, freeing you up for more strategic work.

2. **Time-Consuming Projects That Can Be Broken Down:** Large, time-consuming projects are often excellent opportunities for delegation. Break the project into smaller, manageable parts, and assign those parts to team members who have the skills and capacity to handle them. You'll still maintain oversight, but the majority of the work can be shared.

3. **Tasks That Align with Team Members' Strengths:** Consider delegating tasks that align with your team members' strengths and expertise. If someone on your team has a particular skill set, they're likely to handle related tasks with greater efficiency and higher quality. Delegating tasks that match their abilities benefits you and enhances their job satisfaction. Remember the 70% rule we discussed? Find the talent and delegate the task.
4. **Tasks That Provide Learning Opportunities:** Delegation is also about developing your team. Look for tasks that present opportunities for growth and stretch team members beyond their current comfort zone. These could include managing a small project, leading a meeting, or taking charge of research for a new initiative. In her book Multipliers, Liz Wiseman emphasizes that delegation can be a powerful driver of growth.
5. **Tasks That Don't Require Your Unique Expertise or Authority** A good rule of thumb is to ask yourself, "Does this task require my specific expertise or authority to be completed?" If the answer is no, it's likely something that can be delegated. By delegating these tasks, you free yourself up to focus on the responsibilities that demand your leadership and decision-making abilities.

Now that you are an expert on the types of tasks that are suitable for delegation ***take a moment and grab a pen and paper***. Review the list provided above once more. As you read each number, pause and <u>write down any current activities you have that correspond to that idea</u>. After you've listed all the ideas you can for that number, move on to the next one and repeat the exercise. Now, you have a list of work you do that you can delegate.

Three Levels of Responsibility in Delegation

Tools, tools, and more tools! This chapter is all about showcasing different tools and approaches that will help you think about delegation wholistically. By looking at delegation from different perspectives, you can be more effective, strategic, and, most importantly, intentional.

In the figure below, you see that all activities that can be delegated fall into one of three categories, which we call *Responsibility Levels*. Take a moment to notice the levels and what happens as we move from left to right across the figure.

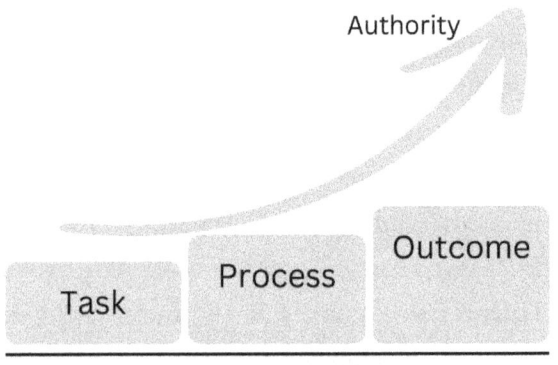

Responsibility Levels

As you can see in the image above, delegation has three distinct responsibility levels: *Task*, *Process*, and *Outcome*. These levels represent different stages of responsibility that you can assign to a team member, depending on their experience, skill, and readiness. Understanding these levels helps ensure that you match the right level of responsibility with the appropriate amount of authority, setting both you and your team members up for success.

1. **Task-Level Responsibility**

    At the task level, delegation is straightforward and focused on a single action or activity. When you delegate at this level, you're essentially demonstrating the task to the team member. This could involve providing step-by-step instructions or showing them how to perform the task in a hands-on way. For example, you might assign a new employee the responsibility of answering the phone, with clear instructions to greet the caller in a specific manner and transfer the call as directed.

Because task-level delegation is so focused, it requires minimal authority and involves only a narrow scope of responsibility. This level of delegation is ideal for new or less-experienced team members who are building foundational skills. By teaching them individual tasks, you help them develop confidence in a controlled environment. Typically, these are tasks that you need to delegate to leverage your time more efficiently. These tasks may be repetitive or distract you from doing your best work.

2. **Process-Level Responsibility**

   When team members are ready to take on more, they can move to process-level responsibility. At this stage, you're not just delegating a single task but an entire system or process. This often involves multiple tasks that need to be coordinated and managed to achieve a specific goal. To clarify the scope of responsibility, it's crucial to provide a *standard operating procedure (SOP)* or similar guidelines. An SOP outlines the process from start to finish, detailing each step and transition point, including where the process may be handed off to someone else.

   For instance, a team member might be responsible for managing the entire customer service process rather than just answering phones. This includes ensuring all calls are handled correctly, interactions meet company standards, and any follow-up actions are completed. Delegating at the process level requires a higher degree of authority because the individual may need to guide others, manage transition points, and make decisions about how the process unfolds. By granting them process-level responsibility, you empower the team members to see beyond individual tasks and take ownership of a complete workflow. This enables them to make meaningful contributions and allows you to step back, knowing the process is in capable hands.

3. **Outcome-Level Responsibility**

    The highest level of responsibility you can delegate is outcome-level responsibility, where a team member is accountable for achieving a specific, measurable result. Unlike task or process delegation, you may not have all the steps or details worked out when delegating an outcome. In this case, you're granting the team member the authority to create the processes and tasks needed to achieve the desired result.

    Outcome-level delegation requires not just authority but also a clear vision. Since you may not have a standard operating procedure or predefined tasks, your role as the leader is to <u>paint a vivid picture of the desired outcome</u>. The team member must fully understand what success looks like, including any key metrics or expectations. For example, you might delegate the goal of increasing customer service-driven sales by 20%. Here, the team member is responsible not just for overseeing a process but for creating the strategy, setting up the necessary tasks, and managing the team to achieve the outcome.

Notice that as you move across the figure from left to right, the authority level required increases.

Leaders who delegate poorly do not understand one of the fundamental tenets of delegation:

> **Success** is not possible in a delegation strategy if the leader only delegates processes or outcomes without delegating the matching level of **AUTHORITY.**

Here is a cautionary tale.

I had a friend ask me to help save his struggling tech company. He was the main investor and head of the board of directors. While discussing my concerns with him, I expressed my thoughts about the company's instability and, more importantly, that the people running the business were extremely inexperienced in both business and the tech industry. My friend kept saying he was stressed and needed me to come in and fix it, whatever it took. So, with some hesitation, I signed on to be the CEO and right the ship.

After several discouraging meetings with the team and discovering it was much worse than I had originally expected, I told my friend we needed to make some staffing changes and let two employees go. "Absolutely not," my friend told me. He told me the two people were related to one of the other main investors and that they could not be let go under any circumstances. The board members would not allow me to make the necessary changes. My friend had made a fundamental mistake in delegating. He gave me the *responsibilities* that come with being the CEO but not the *authority* that is required to create the desired outcome.

After just a few months in the position, despite achieving some small wins, I ultimately decided it was best for me to resign. I recognized that without the ability to bring in a team of experienced and dedicated professionals, the company had little chance of surviving. I left, and the company limped along for another few months and eventually closed. This experience taught me valuable lessons: never assume that a title or position automatically comes with the authority needed to fulfill its responsibilities. I was also reminded as a leader that:

> If I ever delegate an outcome, I must also delegate the necessary authority to maximize the chance of engagement and success.

Now, we have compiled a list of work activities that can be delegated. Review the list and categorize each item by its Responsibility Level. How many on the list are Task Level? How many are Outcome Level? Ask yourself "Do I plan to delegate the appropriate authority for each item on my list?"

Balancing The Matrix

Now you have a list of activities to potentially delegate, and you have qualified them, each with a corresponding level of responsibility. Next we need to add a few more qualifiers to make it clear what activities on our list are the most important. So we will shift our discussion about our delegation strategy to thinking about the level of importance and urgency of our work. We are going to use this approach to help identify how we *actually* spend our time versus how we *could* spend our time. We are going to look at a very famous concept called The Eisenhower Matrix, which former President Dwight D Eisenhower developed during his time in the military. Let's look at its component parts.

Urgency - Ask yourself, "Does this task need immediate attention?" If it's time-sensitive but doesn't align closely with your bigger priorities, it might be something you can pass on. For instance, a quick customer service issue might need fast action, but it doesn't always need you personally. By delegating, you let someone else take on the *responsibility* of handling it promptly, while you stay *accountable* for overall customer satisfaction.

Importance - Consider, "Does this task align with my core responsibilities?" If it's central to your role or contributes directly to long-term goals, it might be something you keep. This area is important for leaders to focus on closely. Do not delegate core responsibilities and core strengths. However, if the task or outcome is truly important to the organization, you want to make sure to delegate to skillful and passionate leaders on your team. Even when you delegate these important activities, remember you may still hold the ultimate *accountability* for the end result. This means staying connected to the progress of the work is important, even if the day-to-day work is someone else's *responsibility*.

Let's take a moment to apply these ideas. We can take them and create a matrix to help us better understand managing our time. For example, administrative tasks like scheduling meetings, organizing reports, or preparing presentations are often time-consuming but don't require your specific expertise. These are perfect candidates for delegation. They may be URGENT, but they are not IMPORTANT. By offloading these *tasks* to a capable team member, you free yourself up to focus on higher-level responsibilities and *outcomes* that drive your organization forward.

The **Eisenhower Matrix** (also discussed in Stephen Covey's *The 7 Habits of Highly Effective People*), divides tasks into four quadrants based on urgency and importance:

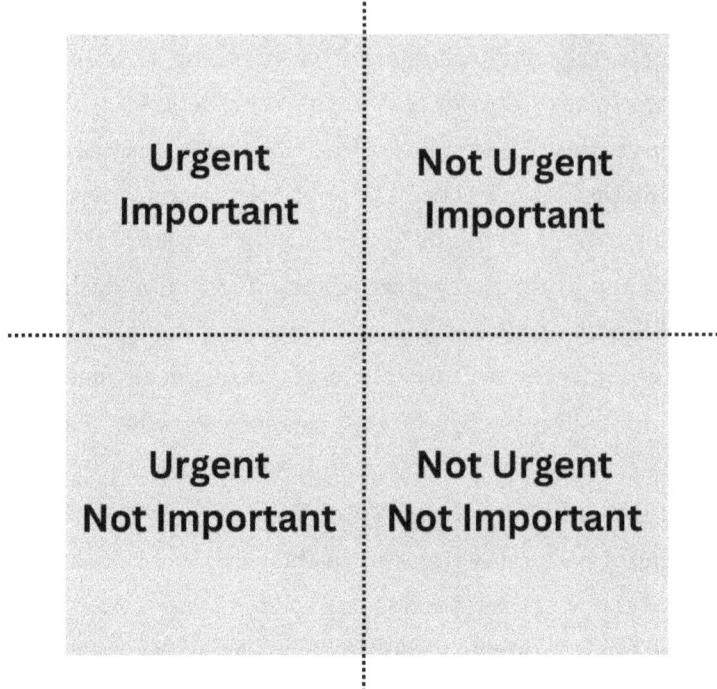

The Eisenhower Matrix

Important and Urgent: These tasks often require your immediate attention. Hopefully, as we delegate and become more proactive in our leadership, these events will decrease over time to a manageable level. They include tasks, processes, or outcomes with deadlines or consequences.

Important but Not Urgent: These tasks are crucial to long-term success and could be some of the most critical activities of an organization's long-term success. Planning, communicating, innovating, and mitigating are all not urgent but very important. Your goal as a leader is to continually increase the amount of time you spend in this quadrant.

Not Important but Urgent: Perfect for delegation, as they demand action but not necessarily from you. These activities can be distractions from more important issues.

Not Important and Not Urgent: These can often be eliminated. As our organizations grow, unfortunately, activities in this category also grow. It's called bureaucracy, which is something as a leader, you should try to eliminate before you delegate.

The last section explored delegation through the lenses of urgency and importance. Consider how you spend your days: **which quadrant receives the most attention, and which one receives the least?** By reflecting on urgency, importance, and responsibility, you can make your delegation more intentional.

> As a leader, your goal should be to delegate with **intention**.

This means prioritizing high-value activities and responsibilities, developing your team, and aligning tasks with the strengths of your team members. Ultimately, the intention is to leverage your role in a way that allows the team or organization to grow, preventing you from becoming a bottleneck.

The Cornerstones of Successful Delegation

Trust is a two-way street in delegation. You need to trust your team members to handle the delegated tasks, and they need to trust that you'll support them and not micromanage them.

> When you delegate correctly to the right team members, you build **trust**.

Here's how you can build trust and accountability through delegation:

- **Set clear expectations**: Make sure your team members know exactly what's expected of them, including deadlines

and outcomes. Be transparent about why you're delegating a particular task.
- **Provide support when needed**: Be available to offer guidance, but avoid hovering or micromanaging. Provide all necessary information, resources, and the authority needed to complete the job.
- **Allow autonomy**: Give them the freedom to complete the task in their own way as long as they meet the desired results. Refer to the Responsibility Levels if you have any questions.
- **Acknowledge success**: Recognize their efforts and celebrate when the task is completed successfully. **Catch your team members doing things right!**
- **Identify process failures**: View mistakes as learning opportunities and use the opportunity to coach and correct the process, not communicate it's a personal failure.

> Research has shown that high-trust organizations are more than 2.5 times more likely to be high-performing organizations (HBR 2016).

By using delegation as a tool to build trust, you're not just improving task management – you're enhancing overall organizational performance. You also create a culture where team members feel empowered to take on new challenges and grow in their roles.

A Strategy Crafting Tool

A helpful tool for making delegation decisions is our **Delegation Matrix**, which helps you categorize tasks based on their urgency, importance, and developmental value. Below is a simple version of it you can create in Excel, or you can download our free Delegation Matrix tool at www.Perforam.com/Caveman.

Activity	Responsibility Level	Urgent & Important	Candidate for Delegation	Skill & Will	Keep / Drop / Delegate

The **first column is your activities**. If you haven't already, take a few minutes and write down all the activities you have created from the last two chapters. If you want to be sure you have all the activities, print the list and keep the list on your desk for the following month to track your work. Add anything that you missed.

Next, write the titles of the next five columns to the right of your list. Here are the titles and possible responses:

Responsibility Level – List if the activity that could be delegated is a task, process, or outcome.

Urgency / Importance – When you do this task, what level of urgency are you operating under? These are the "fires" you put out every day. How important is this task in accomplishing the mission, vision, and values of your team or organization?

Candidate for Delegation – This column will have the name of the individual that you are evaluating as a potential delegation candidate for the activity listed in column one.

Level of Skill and Will – Consider the candidate you mentioned in the previous column. Do they possess a high level of skill related to the work to be completed? We define "high" skill as the ability to perform the task at 70-80% of your capability. If they can achieve this level of performance, we would classify them as having high skill.

Next, evaluate their level of will. View the task from their perspective: Does it provide opportunities for development, allow them to learn a new skill, present a new challenge, add to their responsibilities, or offer some other motivating factor? Have you asked if the task sounds interesting to them? If they express motivation to take on this new work, rate them as having "high will."

Keep, Drop, Delegate – Once you have filled out all the columns and carefully considered your delegation strategy—specifically, the what, when, and who—it is time to decide whether to keep the activity, drop it entirely, or delegate it to the person you have selected.

Once you have completed filling out the list and the information in the matrix, keep it close by because we will return to it later in the book. You should now have a clear understanding of which activities are suitable for delegation. Before we move on to the next chapter and consider the "who" of delegation, let's review our list to ensure that there are no items that shouldn't be delegated.

Red Light, Green Light Responsibilities

This entire book focuses on the art of delegation. However, there are situations where delegation may not be the best choice. Great leaders understand when to retain control over tasks and when to delegate them. It's similar to the children's game "Red Light, Green Light." "Green Light" tasks are those we can delegate, while "Red Light" tasks are those we should keep. If a task requires your direct involvement—either because it is strategically important, involves ownership or accountability, or deals with sensitive information—we categorize it as a "Red Light." Here are some tasks that leaders typically should retain:

1. **Strategic Planning and High-Level Decision-Making:** Your role as a leader involves setting the vision and direction for your team or organization. These high-level decisions—such as shaping company strategy or guiding the team's overall goals—require your direct involvement. While you may seek input from your team, the final decisions often need to be yours. Ask yourself, "What are the highest-order decisions I make in my position that create the greatest impact on my team or organization?" Don't dismiss this point if you are not a CEO. If you lead a team, you are the vision keeper! High-level decision-making activities are those that are associated with any leadership position, from the front line manager to the CEO. As Jim Collins explains in his book *Good to Great*, great leaders know when to stay involved in strategic decision-making while empowering their teams to handle execution.

2. **Performance Reviews and Personnel Matters** Evaluating your team's performance, conducting reviews, and handling personnel issues are sensitive tasks that should typically remain in your hands. While you can delegate aspects of performance tracking, the final responsibility for reviews and development planning usually rests with you. Most people hate giving or receiving performance reviews. Our company, Perforam, reinvented performance reviews for that reason. We call them 5|25 Reviews, and they eliminate all pointless box-checking and "ratings for raises." You can learn more about our work at www.Perforam.com. Delegating feedback to other managers or team leads can be effective, but make sure you stay involved in key decisions that impact your team's development and morale.

3. **Crisis Management** When critical issues arise, your leadership and experience are often necessary to navigate the situation effectively. Crises demand a strong, steady hand, and delegating during these times may not be the best course of action—at least not initially. For example, during a significant organizational change, it's essential for you as the leader to manage communications and ensure that the transition goes smoothly. Once the immediate crisis is managed, you can begin to delegate aspects of the ongoing work.

4. **Building and Maintaining Key Relationships** Whether it's with clients, partners, or key stakeholders, maintaining strategic relationships is often a responsibility that should remain with you. Delegating these interactions could weaken the trust and rapport you've built over time, so it's important to manage these connections personally. However, look at connection points and aspects of the relationship that are not important. Do you personally buy gifts for the client? Maybe you should delegate gift buying to someone else. Do you spend time setting up meetings, scheduling lunches, etc.? Maintaining the relationship is important, but many administrative behind-the-scenes activities can be delegated.

The Keep, Drop, Delegate Exercise

To make your delegation strategy and matrix even more straightforward, try the **Keep, Drop, Delegate** exercise. This is your last column on the matrix. By this time, you have completed steps 1 and 2 and should finish Step 3:

1. **Create Your List of Activities/Responsibilities**
2. **Categorize Each Task**:

- Ownership and core responsibilities.
- Urgency / Importance
- Skill Level / Energy Level
- Responsibility Level

3. **Add the last Column Titled "KDD"**
    - The responses for the KDD are Keep, Drop, or Delegate and are based on the following criteria:
        1. Tasks you can drop or eliminate because they add little value.
        2. Tasks you can delegate to someone else.
        3. Task you keep because you own them, you are world-class at executing them, and they give you energy.

This simple exercise often reveals tasks that you've been holding onto unnecessarily and highlights new opportunities to delegate.

The main takeaway is that strategic delegation not only reduces your workload but also enhances the entire team's performance. Understanding what to delegate is just as crucial as knowing when to do it. Evidence shows aligning tasks with team members' strengths and motivations significantly boosts their performance and engagement (Johnstone, 2000). By delegating tasks that match individual skills and interests, both the leader and the team member benefit: the leader becomes more efficient, while the team member experiences professional growth and satisfaction. By clearly identifying which tasks to delegate and which to retain, you can better align your efforts with the most impactful areas of your leadership role.

As you refine your delegation strategy, remember that it's an ongoing process. Regularly reassess your tasks and responsibilities, and always look for new opportunities to delegate and empower your team. You could even add reviewing your Delegation Matrix to your calendar once a year to make sure to update and change it as your team and responsibilities grow and change.

In the next chapter, we'll explore the crucial question of who to delegate to – because choosing the right person for the task is just as important as choosing the right task to delegate.

CHAPTER 4:
THE "WHO" OF DELEGATION

· · ·

"If you pick the right people and give them the opportunity to spread their wings – and put compensation as a carrier behind it – you almost don't have to manage them."
– Jack Welch, former CEO at General Electric

The Art of Matchmaking in Delegation

Delegation goes beyond simply assigning tasks; it involves identifying the right people or resources to handle them. Think of it like casting actors for a play. You wouldn't randomly assign roles; you would carefully evaluate each actor's strengths, experience, and potential. This same principle applies to delegation. Choosing the right person or resource for each task is essential for success. We will spend more time unpacking how to do this in Chapters 8, 9, and 10.

You might wonder why we refer to both people and "resources" in the context of delegation. Sometimes, we forget that delegation doesn't just include human-to-human handoffs. When considering tasks, processes, or outcomes, you have at least three options for delegation. **You can delegate activities to the wastebasket,**

Artificial Intelligence (AI), or a rockstar. The wastebasket and AI are viable options leaders often overlook when creating their delegation strategy.

The wastebasket symbolizes the deletion of tasks that clutter your day and serve only as distractions. These activities belong to the Not Urgent, Not Important quadrant of the Eisenhower Matrix. Instead of delegating these tasks to someone else, it's best to eliminate them entirely. For instance, you might find yourself spending excessive time scrolling through social media each day. Since this activity is neither urgent nor important, consider removing the apps from your phone to make them less accessible. If that doesn't work, be bold! Cancel your accounts on all but one or two platforms. Clear out activities that are wasting your time by sending them to the wastebasket.

The next option involves delegating a digital task or process to AI or automation tools like Zapier. If you have repetitive digital tasks, consider the possibility of automating some of those processes with cloud-based systems or AI platforms. Properly set up, automation can save time and free individuals from tedious, repetitive tasks. Therefore, broaden your perspective—remember that humans aren't the only option for delegation in the information age.

Finally, if a task, process, or outcome is important and cannot be automated, your best choice is to find someone who is at least 70% capable of handling it. These individuals are your delegation rockstars. They are capable of taking on responsibilities and following through. They require clear direction but do not need constant supervision. They are your high performers and reliable team members.

In this chapter, we will explore how to effectively match tasks with team members and identify who the "rockstars" are on our team, considering their skills, potential, and career goals.

Assessing Skills, Potential, and Career Goals

If you finished the Delegation Matrix we covered in the last chapter, it's time to look at the list of tasks, processes, and outcomes and think about the delegation options. Review the list you created, and when deciding who to delegate to, consider these key factors:

1. **Current skills and knowledge:** What are your team members' existing capabilities? Look for areas where their skills align with the task on the Matrix.
2. **Potential and learning agility:** Sometimes, the best person for a task isn't the most skilled but the one with the most potential to grow into the role. Does an inexperienced team member have potential but needs a chance to prove themselves? What activities would be a good fit?
3. **Career aspirations:** Delegation can be a powerful tool for career development. Consider tasks that align with your team members' long-term goals.
4. **Workstyle and preferences:** Some people thrive on variety, while others prefer routine. Match tasks to individual working styles when possible. We will talk about individual drivers using the Enneagram in Chapters 8,9, and 10.
5. **Current workload and capacity:** Be mindful of your team members' existing responsibilities. Overloading someone can lead to burnout and poor performance.

> A study by Gallup found that **employees who use their strengths every day are six times more likely to be engaged at work.**

By aligning delegated tasks with individual strengths and aspirations, you're not just getting the job done – you're boosting engagement and job satisfaction.

The Skill-Will Matrix: A Delegation Tool

One practical tool to help you determine the right person for the task is the **Skill-Will Matrix**. This model, developed by leadership experts Paul Hersey and Ken Blanchard, categorizes individuals based on their skills and motivation (or will) to take on a task. It can guide you in selecting the best candidates for delegation:

- **High Skill, High Will**: These individuals are your go-to people. They have both the capability and the motivation to take on tasks and run with them. For critical tasks that require expertise and initiative, these are the people you can rely on.
- **High Skill, Low Will**: While these team members have the necessary skills, they may lack motivation or enthusiasm for the task. In these cases, it's important to explore what's holding them back. Is it a lack of interest in the task itself, or is there something else preventing them from being fully engaged?
- **Low Skill, High Will**: These individuals are eager to learn but may lack the experience or knowledge to complete the task independently. <u>This is where delegation can be a great development tool.</u> Assign tasks that allow them to build their skills gradually, offering support and guidance along the way.
- **Low Skill, Low Will**: Individuals in this category may need additional support or motivation. Delegating to them may require more hands-on guidance at first, and it's important to set clear expectations and offer encouragement to help them succeed.

You can add these new quadrants to your Delegation Matrix or download our version for free. This matrix can guide your delegation decisions, helping you match tasks with the right team members and identify areas where additional support or motivation might be needed.

Building a Diverse Delegation Portfolio

Just as a savvy investor diversifies their portfolio, a skilled leader should diversify their delegation. When you delegate tasks to different team members, you spread opportunities for growth, reduce bottlenecks, and improve overall team performance.

By delegating to multiple people, you mitigate the risk of overloading any one individual. If a team member is unavailable or falls behind, others can step in to keep the project moving forward. Also, distributing tasks across your team helps build a well-rounded, versatile workforce. You give more people the opportunity to expand their skill sets, making the team stronger and more resilient in the long run.

Finally, different people bring different perspectives. By delegating tasks to a variety of individuals, you open the door to new ideas and innovative solutions that you might not have considered yourself. It also ensures that your team doesn't become too dependent on any one person. It promotes knowledge-sharing, collaboration, and continuous learning across the team.

Considering Learning Styles and Delegation

People learn and work in different ways. Some are visual learners, others are hands-on, and some prefer detailed written instructions. Understanding these differences can help you delegate more effectively. We will cover this more in the next chapter.

By adapting your delegation style to individual learning preferences, you can enhance understanding and improve outcomes.

The Power of Stretch Assignments

Sometimes, the best person to delegate to isn't the most obvious choice. Stretch assignments – tasks that push people slightly beyond their current capabilities – can be powerful tools for development.

This idea is supported by findings from a study by Korn Ferry, which found that 71% of organizations use stretch assignments for leadership development. These challenging tasks can accelerate learning, boost confidence, and prepare team members for future roles.

When considering stretch assignments:
1. Choose tasks that are challenging but achievable.
2. Provide adequate support and resources.
3. Be clear about expectations and the learning nature of the assignment.
4. Offer regular feedback and guidance.

Remember, the goal of a stretch assignment isn't just task completion – it's growth and development.

Case Study: Jack Welch's Work-Out Program— Delegation in Action

Jack Welch, the legendary former CEO of General Electric, revolutionized leadership with his groundbreaking "Work-Out" program. Recognizing that innovation and agility stem from empowering people at every level of an organization, Welch sought to break down hierarchical barriers and unleash the potential of GE's vast workforce. His philosophy centered on one core idea: the art of leadership is knowing when to step back and let others take ownership.

The Work-Out program was a bold initiative designed to transform GE's culture. Employees and managers from different levels of the company came together in facilitated sessions to identify inefficiencies, propose solutions, and make decisions on the spot. The brilliance of the program lay in its simplicity and immediacy. Instead of ideas being lost in endless layers of approval, managers were required to accept or reject recommendations during the sessions—or commit to a timeline for further exploration. This created an unprecedented level of accountability and trust.

Welch believed that decision-making should happen at the lowest appropriate level in the organization. By delegating authority and pushing responsibility closer to where the work was being done, he empowered employees to feel ownership of their contributions." "Leaders celebrate ideas, remove obstacles, and give others the freedom to execute," Welch often emphasized, showcasing his commitment to removing bureaucratic roadblocks.

The results were transformative. Employees felt heard and motivated, inefficiencies were rapidly identified and resolved, and GE became a more agile and innovative organization. Under Welch's leadership, the company's value skyrocketed, and the Work-Out program became a defining feature of his tenure. By delegating not just tasks but decision-making power, Welch cultivated a culture of trust, accountability, and empowerment.

The lesson for modern leaders is profound: delegation isn't just about offloading work; it's about building a culture where people feel trusted and equipped to make meaningful contributions. Welch's approach demonstrated that when employees are empowered to take ownership, organizations become stronger, more efficient, and more innovative.

The Ongoing Nature of Delegation Decisions

Choosing who to delegate tasks to is not a one-time decision. Selecting the right person for a delegated task often depends on the trust and rapport established within the team. The research team Schriesheim, Neider, and Scandura (1998) conducted studies that reveal the importance of leader-member exchange (LMX) in the delegation process. Their findings indicate that strong, trust-based relationships between leaders and team members lead to smoother delegation and better outcomes. When leaders invest time in building these connections, they create a foundation for mutual understanding and shared success.

To whom should you delegate tasks on your team? To the person who trusts you. But how can you increase trust among your team members? By delegating responsibilities. This creates a virtuous cycle: the more you delegate, the more your team members will trust you. As their trust in you grows, your delegation will become even more effective and the more your team will grow.

As your team members grow and develop, their capabilities and interests will change. Regular check-ins and performance discussions can help you stay attuned to these changes and adjust your delegation strategy accordingly. You may need to periodically update your Delegation Matrix.

Consider implementing a system for tracking delegated tasks and their outcomes. This can help you identify patterns, recognize development opportunities, and refine your delegation decisions over time. We created a development framework system at Perforam that helps manage not only delegated tasks but also the development of every person on your team. Check it out at www.Perforam.com to learn more about our performance management tools.

As you move forward in your delegation journey, remember that matching the right task with the right person is both an art and a science. It requires a deep understanding of your team members, a strategic approach to task allocation, and a willingness to adapt and learn from each delegation experience.

In the next chapter, we'll dive into the "how" of delegation, exploring a technique that we developed that is simple, helpful, and makes it easy to transfer responsibilities and ensure successful outcomes.

CHAPTER 5:
THE "HOW" OF DELEGATION

...

> "Leadership is not about being in charge. It is about taking care of those in your charge."
> – Simon Sinek

When I was stressed and riding on the lawn mower listening to the podcast, I had forgotten the delegation method they outlined before I even made it back inside. That is how the Caveman Method is different. Once you hear it, you won't forget it! It's time for the most famous delegation tactic from the prehistoric era.

The Art and Simplicity of Neanderthals
Picture a caveman teaching his son to hunt. He doesn't hand over a spear and say, "Good luck!" Instead, he demonstrates, guides, and gradually lets his son take the lead. This instinctive approach to teaching is the inspiration behind the **Caveman Delegation Method**.

In this chapter, we'll explore this powerful technique for delegation, breaking it down into four simple steps that can transform the way you transfer responsibilities to your team. By gradually transferring responsibility to your team members, you not only ensure the successful completion of tasks but also help them develop confidence and competence over time. The key is to follow a structured, step-by-step process that builds their skills while maintaining quality.

Understanding the Caveman Delegation Method

The Caveman Delegation Method is a structured approach to delegation that emphasizes the gradual transfer of responsibility. It's designed to build confidence, ensure quality, and promote learning. Here are the four steps:

Step 1: Me Do (Demonstration)
Step 2: Me Do, You Watch (Observation)
Step 3: You Do, Me Watch (Supervised, Hands-On, Practice)
Step 4: You Do Up To (Graduated Autonomy)

Let's dive into each step and see how you can apply them in your delegation practice.

Step 1: Me Do

In this initial stage, you perform the task yourself while explaining each step clearly. It's like the caveman telling his son why they go hunting and showing him the prize when he comes back from the hunt. It's essential to take the time to explain ***not only what you're doing but also why you're doing it that way***. This provides valuable context and helps your team member understand the reasoning behind your actions.

Key Actions:

- Explain why the task, process, or outcome is important.
- Highlight potential challenges and how you overcome them.

Example: Imagine you are delegating the task of creating a monthly sales report. In the "Me Do" stage, you would create the report yourself. You might express your excitement to future candidates for delegation by saying that the team needed a new sales report to provide greater visibility and insights into the organization's sales funnel.

Step 2: Me Do, You Watch

In this stage, you perform the task again, but this time your team member observes closely. It's like the caveman repeating the hunting demonstration but showing him how to hold the spear and aim at the target. It's an opportunity for them to see the process in action and ask questions to clarify any uncertainties. This step is all about deepening their understanding of the task before they attempt it themselves.

Key Actions:
- Break the task down into clear, manageable steps.
- Encourage questions and clarifications throughout the process.
- Point out nuances and decision points.
- Explain your thought process as you work.

Example: You create another sales report, but this time your team member is watching over your shoulder. You take time to narrate each step as they watch: "First, I pull the data from our CRM system. Then, I organize it in this spreadsheet template..." You might say, "Notice how I'm filtering out these specific entries? That's because..."

Educational psychology research backs this up—people often learn best when they can see a task modeled for them. The concept of "modeling" in educational psychology, which has been shown to be an effective teaching method. By seeing the task performed correctly, your team member is more likely to replicate it effectively. This stage is also referred to as "guided observation." This observational learning is supported by social learning theory, which emphasizes the importance of watching others to acquire new behaviors.

Step 3: You Do, Me Watch

Now it's time for your team member to take the reins while you supervise. Like the caveman watching his son throw his first spear, you're there to provide guidance, offer feedback, and ensure the task is being done correctly.

Key Actions:
- Allow the team member to perform the task independently.
- Provide guidance only when necessary.
- Offer constructive feedback and encouragement.

Example: Your team member creates the sales report while you observe. You might say, "Great job on organizing the data. Have you considered including a breakdown by product category?"

This step incorporates the principle of "guided practice" from instructional design, which helps learners build confidence and competence. Guided practice is critical in building both competence and confidence, allowing the individual to refine their approach based on real-time feedback.

Step 4: You Do Up To

The final step is to give your team members **autonomy** to complete the task independently but with clear boundaries and checkpoints. It's like the caveman letting his son go on a hunt alone for smaller animals and checking in at agreed times.

Key Actions:
- Define clear expectations and boundaries for the task.
- Establish checkpoints for progress updates.
- Provide a safety net for questions or issues.

Example: You might say, "I'd like you to handle the monthly sales report moving forward. Let's check in after you've completed the first two sections to make sure everything's on track."

This approach aligns with the concept of "scaffolding" in educational psychology, where support is gradually removed as the learner becomes more competent. By the end of this process, your team member should be fully capable of handling the task independently, with confidence and proficiency.

The Science Behind the Caveman Method

Teams that go through our training and begin implementing the Caveman Method start including into their company's lexicon. You here people give updates in meetings by saying "We have got to move him from You Do, Me Watch to You Do Up To." Immediately everyone knows where they are in the handoff and what needs to happen next.

The Caveman Delegation Method is not only intuitive but also grounded in established principles from learning theory and psychology. This method utilizes several well-researched strategies for skill development. For example, observational learning is crucial in Steps 1 and 2, where the team member observes and absorbs the process. This approach aligns with findings on modeling and observation, which have proven to be highly effective in acquiring new skills.

As the learner progresses, Steps 3 and 4 introduce active learning, allowing them to engage directly with the task and improve their retention and understanding. Furthermore, the

Caveman Method reflects the "I do, we do, you do" framework commonly used in education, which gradually shifts responsibility to the learner.

The Leader-Member Exchange Theory emphasizes the importance of tailoring leadership approaches to individual team members(Graen and Uhl-Bien's 1995) . Applying this to the Caveman Delegation Method means adapting each step to the capabilities and confidence of the person taking on the responsibility. This customization ensures that delegation fosters trust, competence, and ownership.

The gradual release of responsibility supports the concept of scaffolding, a principle in cognitive psychology where support is slowly removed as the learner gains confidence. Together, these components create a robust, research-backed approach to developing competency through delegation.

Caveman + The Three Responsibility Levels

The Caveman Delegation Method isn't just a one-size-fits-all approach. Different types of responsibilities require subtle variations in how we apply our delegation strategy. *Think of it like cooking – the basic technique might remain the same, but you'll adjust your approach depending on whether you're making a delicate soufflé or a hearty stew. Earlier in Chapter 3, we introduced the three Levels of Responsibility: Task, Process, and Outcome. Every activity you delegate will typically fall into one of these categories, and understanding these levels helps you tailor your delegation strategy. Now, let's combine this framework with the Caveman Delegation Method to see how the approach adapts for each level. While the methodology remains the same, its application shifts to fit the scope of responsibility.*

Caveman + Tasks

When delegating tasks, the Caveman Method is intuitive and straightforward. You are physically doing the task in Step 1, demonstrating it in a hands-on way. In Step 2, *Me Do, You Watch*, you show the person how to perform the task, breaking it into clear, actionable steps. In Step 3, *You Do, Me Watch*, you observe the person performing the task, providing guidance and feedback as needed. Finally, in Step 4, *You Do Up To*, you give the person autonomy, outlining specific boundaries for when to seek help or escalate issues.

For example, imagine you are delegating the task of counting equipment on mechanical drawings to develop an estimate. You might demonstrate how to count the equipment and explain what to look for. In Step 4, you could set boundaries, such as, "Only call me if the equipment count exceeds a certain number, if it includes rare equipment, or if the configuration is confusing." This approach ensures the person understands the task and the limits of their autonomy while freeing you to focus on higher-value activities.

Caveman + Process

Delegating a process is similar to delegating tasks but involves additional steps to clarify and coordinate a broader scope of responsibility. Processes often span multiple tasks and may require input from several people, especially in growing organizations where no one previously owned the entire process. Here's how the Caveman Method applies to processes:

- **Step 1: Me Do (or We Do):** In many cases, no single person is managing the entire process when you start. For example, different team members might handle parts of the process. In this phase, it's important to bring everyone involved together to clarify the *why* behind the delegation and establish a shared understanding of the process. The leader facilitates these discussions and gathers insights to create a clear picture of how the process currently works.

- **Step 2: Me Do, You Watch:** This stage begins with creating a detailed *Standard Operating Procedure (SOP)*. The SOP should outline the entire process, including start and end points, steps, transitions, and handoffs. The person assuming responsibility for the process should shadow team members currently handling individual steps, comparing the current practices with the SOP. This helps them understand the process wholistically and identify any gaps or inefficiencies.

- **Step 3: You Do, Me Watch:** At this stage, the person begins managing the process according to the SOP. Communication is critical here, as they integrate all the steps and refine how the process operates. Feedback from team members involved in the handoffs is essential to ensure a smooth transition. The leader should monitor progress and provide support as the person adjusts and optimizes the process.

- **Step 4: You Do Up To:** Once the SOP is finalized and the process runs smoothly, the person assumes full responsibility. At this point, it's important to clarify their authority within the process—what decisions they can make, what adjustments they're allowed to implement, and where their authority ends. Managing a process requires more authority than managing individual tasks, so ensuring alignment between responsibility and authority is key.

For example, consider a scenario where you delegate the estimation process in your organization. Previously, an admin entered bid data and communicated with clients, another person counted equipment, and a third person assigned values. You bring the team together to discuss their roles, create a comprehensive SOP, and transition the entire estimation process to a single person. This new process owner might adjust roles (e.g., deciding to communicate directly with clients rather than relying on the admin) and is given the authority to make key decisions, such as pricing the estimates.

Caveman + Outcome

Delegating outcomes takes the Caveman Method to its most abstract and strategic level. Unlike tasks or processes, outcomes often lack predefined steps or an SOP. Here, the focus shifts from managing specifics to aligning on vision and results.

- **Step 1: Me Do:** At the outcome level, *Me Do* involves creating the vision or concept. For example, you might land a project, envision a new division, or decide to expand your product line. Your primary role in this step is clarifying and articulating the *why* behind the desired outcome—why it matters, why it's worth pursuing, and why the person you're delegating to is the right fit to lead it.
- **Step 2: Me Do, You Watch:** This step is about transferring the vision in as much detail as possible. Think of it as *Me See, You See*. Share not only the outcome you want but also any experiential knowledge, insights, or potential pitfalls. The goal is to give the person a clear mental picture of success and prepare them for the challenges ahead. This might include sharing past experiences, lessons learned, or strategic guidance.
- **Step 3: You Do, Me Watch:** Here, the focus shifts to setting targets, KPIs, or milestones. Unlike tasks or processes, you're not watching individual actions; instead, you're monitoring progress toward the outcome through

measurable indicators. Your role is to provide support, remove roadblocks, and offer feedback to keep the person aligned with the vision. Regular check-ins help ensure progress without micromanaging.

- **Step 4: You Do Up To:** In the final stage, the person assumes full responsibility for achieving the outcome. This requires a clear understanding of their authority—what decisions they can make, whether they can reorganize teams or processes, hire or fire staff, and so on. Misaligned authority and responsibility at this stage can derail even the best intentions, so clarity is critical.

For example, let's say you've delegated the entire estimation process to someone, and they've excelled. You now want to delegate the outcome of increasing company profits by 10% over the next year. To achieve this, you choose to give them visibility into profit and loss statements and the authority to adjust billing rates. By empowering them with both responsibility and authority, you can delegate an outcome and position them to meet the challenge successfully.

Overcoming Challenges in the Caveman Method

While the Caveman Delegation Method is powerful, it does come with some challenges. Implementing it can initially feel time-consuming, as the gradual transition of responsibility requires patience and dedication. However, reframing the process as an investment of time essential to long-term success can help maintain a positive outlook on the process.

Another potential hurdle is resistance to change. Team members accustomed to more directive leadership styles may hesitate to embrace this approach. In such cases, it's helpful to emphasize the developmental benefits of the Caveman Method, underscoring how it fosters independence and enhances their skills.

Overreliance on support can sometimes hinder individuals from achieving full autonomy. To address this issue, gradually increasing the time between check-ins can help foster confidence and self-sufficiency. Another effective strategy is to set deadlines for each stage of progress. For example, stating, "Our goal is to move from Stage 3 to Stage 4 within three months," makes it clear that team members need to be attentive, as the support will not be available indefinitely.

For particularly complex tasks, breaking down the responsibilities into smaller, more manageable components can make the transition smoother. By acknowledging and addressing these challenges, leaders can implement the Caveman Method effectively and promote growth within their teams.

Measuring Success in the Caveman Method

How do you know if your delegation using this method has been successful? Here are some indicators to look for:

- **Task proficiency**: The team member can complete the task efficiently and effectively without supervision.
- **Confidence level**: The individual feels comfortable taking on the task independently.
- **Knowledge transfer**: The team member can explain the task process to others.
- **Innovation**: The individual starts suggesting improvements or efficiencies in the process.
- **Time savings**: You spend less time on the task and related supervision.

Consider implementing a feedback loop where you and the team member regularly discuss the delegation process and outcomes. As you incorporate the Caveman Delegation Method into your leadership toolkit, remember that, like caveman, the key is patience, persistence, and adaptability. With practice, you'll find this method not only makes your delegation more effective but also contributes to a culture of learning and growth within your team.

Congratulations! You are now thinking and seeing the world like a caveman! We hope that you can use the simplistic language of this approach to revolutionize the way your team speaks about the delegation process. In the next chapter, we will cover some best practices that will complement your new Neanderthal swagger.

CHAPTER 6:
DELEGATION DESIGNED FOR SUCCESS

...

> "Surround yourself with the best people you can find, delegate authority, and don't interfere as long as the policy you've decided upon is being carried out."
> **- Ronald Reagan**

You've put in the hard work to master the art of delegation – now it's time to assess the impact. After all, how will you know if your efforts are paying off if you don't have a way to measure success?

You are already an expert in delegation, but in this chapter, we will cover some best practices and tools to increase the likelihood of success. This isn't a Ron Co. commercial for a rotisserie chicken. When delegating, you can't "Set it and forget it!" It's about creating an environment, systems, and processes that your team needs to be successful and drive better business outcomes.

As you gradually move through the Caveman process and hand over more responsibility in the delegation process, it's important to be honest about the progress.

> It's not about perfection; it's about progress.

We have put together a list of questions you can ask yourself or your team as you are moving through the delegation process to know if the work has been delegated successfully.

Questions That Show Your Delegation is Successful
- Does the high-quality work align with the overall vision and contribute to broader organizational goals?
- Does the work produced consistently meet or exceed expectations?
- Do team members seem more invested in the outcomes of their tasks?
- Are they taking initiative beyond the delegated work?
- Has your workload decreased while your team's output has remained consistent—or even improved?
- Are team members able to take on more challenging responsibilities as a result of the tasks you've delegated?
- Have team members developed new skills or expertise in areas they didn't have before?
- Are you able to focus more on high-level strategic decisions rather than being caught up in day-to-day tasks?
- Do team members proactively report on progress?
- Are team members taking ownership of their successes and failures?

Why are these questions important? Measuring the success of delegation is essential for improving leadership strategies. Research demonstrates how both leaders' and followers' perceptions of delegation outcomes influence satisfaction and effectiveness (Drescher 2017). By incorporating regular feedback loops and performance metrics, leaders can ensure that delegation not only achieves its immediate goals but also promotes long-term team growth and development. Clear communication and well-defined expectations are crucial to this process.

Spend some time reflecting on the questions above. If the answers to the questions are lower than the acceptable standard, before blaming any individuals, see if you can find areas we covered above that were not in place. Was there a solid strategy in place? Did we choose the right time to delegate? Was the person we chose to do the work the best fit? Did we successfully transition the work using the Caveman method? As MJ would say, "I am starting with the man in the mirror…"

Having covered key questions to assess our delegation efforts, we can now dive into the nature of the work we are delegating and ideas on how to enhance its success.

The D.O.S. Framework

Delegation, as we've explored, is not just an act of offloading tasks; it's a thoughtful strategy that requires clarity, intention, and a design that aligns with your team's capabilities and organizational goals. To elevate this process further, we can use Dan Sullivan's D.O.S. framework—an elegant tool that enhances planning, decision-making, and execution in leadership.

D.O.S., which stands for Dangers, Opportunities, and Strengths, allows leaders to evaluate and fine-tune delegation by focusing on three essential elements: mitigating risks, capitalizing on growth potential, and leveraging team members' unique capabilities. When applied to delegation, the D.O.S. framework provides a structured way to ensure that tasks are aligned with goals, challenges are anticipated, and team members are empowered to deliver success.

This method fits perfectly with the Caveman Delegation Method by adding a strategic lens to the "why" and "what" of delegation. Together, these approaches not only ensure smooth transitions of responsibility but also optimize long-term outcomes.

Let's break down how the D.O.S. framework helps you craft delegation strategies that mitigate dangers, unlock opportunities, and amplify strengths. At its core, the D.O.S. framework focuses on three critical elements:

1. **Dangers**: What are the risks, challenges, or barriers that could arise if a task isn't managed effectively? These dangers could include missed deadlines, overwork, or strategic misalignment.
2. **Opportunities**: What potential for growth, learning, or improvement could delegation unlock? Delegating the right responsibilities can empower team members, expand their skill sets, and improve overall efficiency.
3. **Strengths**: What unique abilities, talents, or resources do you and your team possess that can be leveraged to achieve success? Aligning tasks with individual strengths increases effectiveness and fosters engagement.

You might be wondering, "Can I use this tool before I delegate when I'm putting together my Delegation Matrix?" You're absolutely right! This tool can provide an additional perspective or framework to filter your delegation activities and candidates. However, we believe that systematically addressing these elements through the delegation process from start to finish is even more beneficial for both you and your new delegate. This approach opens up meaningful discussions and helps the team member in their new role identify key challenges, opportunities to seize, and strengths to leverage to succeed in their responsibilities. Let's explore how the D.O.S. framework can enhance the delegation process through a detailed and practical example.

Example: Delegating the Management of a New Product Launch

Imagine you're leading a team responsible for launching a new product. This project involves creating marketing campaigns, coordinating with sales teams, and preparing a product demonstration event. As a leader, your time is stretched thin, and you realize it's impossible to manage every aspect yourself. So you delegate a lot of responsibilities to your team members. Let's look at applying the D.O.S. framework and how it helps give your new delegates direction.

1. Identifying Dangers: Building a Foundation of Trust

Every delegation decision carries inherent risks, whether it's missed deadlines, inefficiencies, or misalignment with strategic objectives. Proactively identifying dangers ensures that you have a plan to mitigate potential issues before they arise.

For example, if you delegate a project to a team member who lacks experience preparing a product demonstration, the danger is that they may feel overwhelmed, underperform, or require excessive oversight. To address this, you could pair them with a mentor, provide initial training, or establish clear check-ins to monitor progress. Maybe even run through the entire demonstration well in advance of meeting your customer. One reason that the D.O.S. System is so effective is that it aligns the team around potential dangers and helps everyone become more comfortable about recognizing them and ideate about how to mitigate or eliminate the dangers.

2. Seizing Opportunities: Turning Delegation into Development

Delegation isn't just about getting things done—it's an opportunity to grow your team and expand their capabilities. By identifying opportunities within the tasks you're delegating, you can align responsibilities with individual development goals.

For example, consider the situation where your team is launching a new product. Delegating the marketing strategy to a rising leader presents an opportunity for them to develop strategic thinking skills. Similarly, assigning financial oversight to another team member could help them gain exposure to budgeting and forecasting.

When using D.O.S. with the Caveman Method, you can incorporate developmental opportunities into the "You Do, Me Watch" phase by allowing team members to experiment, take risks, and learn under your guidance before fully owning the task.

3. Leveraging Strengths: Matching Tasks with Talent

Perhaps the most powerful element of the D.O.S. framework is its emphasis on leveraging strengths. Delegation is most effective when responsibilities align with team members' unique abilities—those tasks they're naturally skilled at and energized by. This approach not only ensures quality outcomes but also boosts engagement and job satisfaction.

Imagine you're assigning tasks for the product launch. One team member excels in creative thinking—delegate the branding and campaign design to them. Another has meticulous attention to detail—entrusts them with compliance and legal reviews. By playing to their strengths, you not only elevate the project's success but also create a more motivated and confident team.

After you delegate a task, having conversations about strengths is very important. When you are watching the new person or listening to them describe the new work, are they excited, nervous, exhausted, exhilarated, or apathetic? Make sure to ask them if they feel like their strengths align with the responsibility. If they don't, you might be setting them up for burnout at best and failure at worst.

Cultivating Alignment with the D.O.S. Framework

A key strength of the D.O.S. framework is that it fosters alignment between leaders and their teams. By identifying dangers, you proactively address obstacles that might hinder success before, during, and after the project. By focusing on opportunities, you inspire a sense of purpose and possibility. And by emphasizing strengths, you build confidence and engagement within your team.

It's also important to revisit these elements periodically as the project progresses. Check-in with your team to assess whether any new dangers have emerged, new opportunities have arisen, or strengths have evolved. This iterative approach ensures that delegation remains dynamic and responsive to changing circumstances.

The D.O.S. framework adds depth and strategic clarity to the delegation process. By addressing dangers, you minimize risks and create a safety net for your team. By focusing on opportunities, you unlock growth and development for individuals and the organization. And by leveraging strengths, you align tasks with talent, ensuring optimal outcomes.

When integrated with the Caveman Delegation Method, D.O.S. becomes a powerful tool for designing delegation that drives success. Using Caveman and D.O.S. in concert transforms delegation from a reactive necessity to a proactive strategy, helping you build a resilient, capable team. As we move forward, the next section will explore the importance of investing in training as a key component of sustainable delegation.

Invest in Training

When we first added this section to the book's outline, I nearly took it out. I worried that most readers would glance at the title and think, "Duh." The idea that leaders should invest in training typically gets nods of approval, so why include it? The truth is, many leaders struggle to move from the mindset of "That sounds good" to actually implementing "This is how I train my team." If you look around your team and notice no one can handle a specific task, it's clear that there's a training issue.

Investing in training takes time, and it can be tempting to just do the work yourself. However, think of training as an investment—not just in your team members, but also in your own workload. Over time, the effort you put into training will pay off as your team members become capable of handling responsibilities on their own.

During my first month leading a technical service organization, I had the chance to meet various office leaders across the Southeast. They were impressive—smart, punctual, detail-oriented, and committed to excellence and professionalism. I thought, "This job is going to be easy!" However, upon meeting the non-leadership team members in my second month, I encountered a different reality. Some of the team members were much less professional and lacked the same commitment to excellence. One person even yelled profanity at me when I suggested the importance of coaching and development. Needless to say, he is no longer with the organization.

In this organization, the issue wasn't with the team leaders; the real problem was the huge gap between the top leader and the second-in-command—about the size of the Grand Canyon! Many leaders might not see this as a big deal. After all, if the top leaders are great, what could be wrong? The challenge became apparent shortly after I took on my role, when one of the leaders moved to a new city to open another office. The #2 leader left behind wasn't capable of managing the operations effectively. Luckily, we had other leaders to rely on until the position could be filled.

Effective delegation requires alignment in values, capabilities, and knowledge of the work. Too often, leaders wait until there's a crisis, throw someone into a new role, and call it delegation, saying, "We train using the trial-by-fire approach." Look out below! We just dropped another Delegation Bomb! Brace for impact! This approach resembles a Neanderthal method more than our Caveman Delegation method! Fortunately, there's a better way. Proactive training is essential to delegating effectively. In the case of the service company, we quickly focused on developing our #2 leaders. As soon as we did this, something remarkable happened: the #1 leaders who trained their #2, found their jobs became much easier.

Delegation as a Learning Process

When most people think about delegation, they often overlook the idea of creating a learning environment. However, effective leaders do just that by ensuring that team members feel supported while also having the freedom to resolve challenges independently. This starts with clear communication. When you delegate tasks for development, it's essential to explain why the task is important and what the learning goals are. Let your team members know what you hope they will gain from the experience and demonstrate how you plan to apply the Caveman method. This level of clarity helps them appreciate the task's importance beyond just completing it.

Support is crucial throughout the delegation process. Development takes time, and you want to create experiences that build confidence and awareness. Be available to answer questions and provide guidance, but avoid hovering. Your role is to be a safety net, ensuring that individuals have the necessary resources to succeed without taking over their tasks.

Offering feedback during the process is also vital. Feedback plays a significant role in successful delegation using the Caveman method. Regular check-ins allow you to share constructive feedback, recognize small achievements, and tackle any issues before they escalate. Feedback may vary at each step. For instance, in Step 2, you might ask questions like, "Do you understand what I just did?" or "What did you notice about my approach?" These questions aim to check for understanding and clarity. As you progress to Step 3, the feedback shifts to focus on their experience. You might ask, "Did anything surprise you about the task?" or "Do you feel confident doing this on your own?" This encourages them to reflect on their growing confidence. In the final step, your questions will change again, focusing on accountability and innovation, such as asking, "Are you meeting the project deadlines?" or "What improvements can we make in our process?"

After completing all four steps of the Caveman method, take the time to debrief. Ask the individual about their learning experiences, the challenges they faced, and how they might tackle similar tasks in the future. This reflection is a key part of their development, reinforcing the lessons learned and preparing them for future growth.

Stretch Assignments and Skill Development

One of the best ways to promote growth through delegation is by giving out stretch assignments. A lot of leaders miss the opportunity to use delegation as a way to push their team members into areas where they might feel a bit out of their depth. These tasks require someone to tap into skills they might not realize they have, forcing them to learn and grow in order to succeed.

Unlike a "Delegation Bomb," where you toss someone into a chaotic situation without any training and expect them to fix it, stretch assignments are much more thoughtful and planned for everyone involved. The key to a good stretch assignment is finding that sweet spot where you challenge the individual without overwhelming them. Sometimes, a leader might spot a hidden talent in a team member that they themselves don't even know exists.

Stretch assignments are intentional ways that leaders move people forward into greater responsibility. It's a delicate balance—too much challenge can lead to frustration, while too little may not provide the growth opportunities they need.

In the beginning of the book, I talked about running a venture-funded startup for a few years and how crucial it was for me to delegate. A few months into my role, I decided it was time to make my first hire. I needed someone organized who could handle a lot of changes quickly. I wanted someone who could juggle multiple tasks at once. Fortunately, I hit the jackpot with my first hire—let's call her Julie. In her mid-20s, she had some solid experience working at a marketing firm and was super excited about this new opportunity. Right off the bat, she helped me balance the workload as our team expanded.

That year, our marketing budget was around $750,000. We were working with three different marketing companies, and money was flying out the door. I needed to ensure that our marketing spending was well-managed. At that point, our reports were mostly manual since we hadn't fully set up our accounting systems. Julie had mentioned she had some extra capacity and wanted to take on more responsibility, so I thought this project could be a perfect fit for her. With her marketing background, understanding of our strategy, and overall capability, I figured this would be a slam dunk stretch assignment.

The good news? I was really thoughtful about who to delegate to and when, and Julie also agreed it was a great opportunity for her. The bad news? I was still early in my leadership journey and had no clue about things like Caveman Delegation or any other delegation techniques. After a great discussion, I even promoted her to oversee all our marketing efforts. In her new role, she was supposed to create a monthly report in Excel and set up a meeting to go over our ad spending and marketing results each month. Sounded fantastic, right?

At least, it did to me! I thought I was setting up this awesome position that would give me insight into our entire marketing strategy and provide valuable data to share with the board of directors each month. But that's not quite how it turned out. When we sat down for our first meeting, I was pumped. I couldn't wait to see all the amazing data she had compiled. Instead, she showed me some confusing charts and started reading from her notes about conversations with the marketing companies. Then she pulled up her browser to show me some web results. I was a bit surprised this first meeting didn't exactly meet my expectations—especially since Julie usually exceeded them.

So, we had a chat about it, and I realized something important: Julie wasn't really prepared to build a solid Excel dashboard. She didn't have much experience with Excel, but she didn't mention it in our first meeting because she wanted to impress me in her new role and didn't want to let me down. She was thinking, "How hard can it be, right?"

It also hit me that I hadn't communicated clearly about what I actually wanted to see and how I wanted it presented. I fell into the trap of thinking I could delegate by just reading minds. I handed off the task based on what was in my head but failed to explain it in detail to Julie. She felt disappointed because her work wasn't what I needed, and I was frustrated because, as her boss, I set her up to fail.

The good news? We bounced back pretty quickly. I learned a lot about delegating challenging tasks and got the chance to teach Julie some Excel skills along the way. We worked together on the report for the next month until we nailed it, and after that, she took the lead and did an awesome job. Turns out we were using the Caveman method without even realizing it!

One big takeaway is that good intentions don't always equal good delegation. As a leader, if what you've delegated comes back not quite right, look at how well you delegated before pointing fingers and coaching the team member.

Another important lesson is that stretch assignments can really boost confidence. When a team member rises to the challenge and nails a tough task, it builds their belief in what they can do. Over time, these little wins add up, turning them into a more confident and capable team member ready for even bigger responsibilities. Julie went from being a marketing assistant at a small local company to managing a $750,000 marketing budget and department in just one year.

> When you stretch your people, you will be shocked at what they can achieve.

Defining Delegation KPIs

Now that we have covered one of my not-so-great moments delegating as a leader, we need to cover one of the ways that could have made it better. Defining Key Performance Indicators (KPIs), when moving through the delegation process. This section helps leaders pause and think "How do I measure if we are achieving the 'why' of my delegation?" As leaders, we need to hold ourselves accountable for the original vision we had when we decided we needed to delegate. Please note there's no one-size-fits-all approach. The right KPIs will depend on your delegation goals, your team's dynamics, and the specific challenges you're hoping to address.

That said, here are some common metrics to consider when delegating:

1. **Time Savings:** Track how much time you're able to reclaim by delegating tasks. This could be measured in hours per week or month.
2. **Team Productivity:** Look at overall team output, such as the number of projects completed or the quality of deliverables.
3. **Employee Engagement:** Monitor factors like job satisfaction, retention rates, and the level of initiative shown by your team members.
4. **Organizational Efficiency:** Evaluate metrics like process turnaround times, error rates, and cost savings achieved through delegation.
5. **Succession Planning:** Consider how well your delegation efforts are preparing team members for future leadership roles.
6. **Task Completion and Quality of Work** The most immediate indicator of delegation success is whether tasks are being completed on time and to the expected standard of quality.
7. **Development of Team Members' Skills** One of the long-term indicators of delegation success is the development of your team's skills. Delegation should serve as an opportunity for growth.
8. **Reduction in Your Stress Levels** Delegation should relieve some of the stress and pressure you face as a leader. If you find that your stress levels are decreasing because

you're no longer overburdened with tasks, that's a clear sign that delegation is improving your ability to manage your workload.

9. **Improved Team Accountability** Delegation should foster a culture of accountability within your team. When responsibilities are clearly defined and ownership is assigned, team members are more likely to take accountability for their work.

If leaders really grasp their delegation KPIs at the start of the Caveman Delegation Method, it'll make it way simpler to see if the effort is actually hitting the mark after the delegation is done. So, take a moment to check out your Delegation Matrix. What are the KPIs for the tasks you're planning to pass on?

Gathering Feedback and Assessing Growth

Quantitative metrics are important, but they only tell part of the story. To get a more holistic view of your delegation's success, it's crucial to gather feedback from both your team members and key stakeholders.

We have already discussed setting up check-ins with your team. Ask them how they're feeling about the tasks and responsibilities you've delegated, and listen for any concerns or challenges they're facing. This can help you identify areas where you need to provide more support or adjust your approach.

You can also incorporate delegation-specific questions into your team's performance reviews. We actually created our own solution called, **5|25 Reviews** because <u>most people hate performance reviews</u>! During a 5|25 one of the areas you focus time on is alignment. Having a 5|25 or an old-fashioned performance review is a great time to find out how your team members feel their skills and capabilities have grown as a result of the opportunities you've provided. This can help you identify potential future leaders and create alignment of roles and responsibilities within your team.

Celebrating Successes and Sharing Lessons Learned

As you track your delegation KPI metrics and gather feedback, be sure to celebrate your team's successes. **Recognize** their hard work, **acknowledge** their growth, and **showcase** their achievements. This not only boosts morale but also reinforces the value of delegation and empowerment. I cannot stress this enough.

> We repeat what we reward. Always remember to catch people doing the right thing and offer high praise.

At the same time, don't be afraid to reflect on any setbacks or challenges you've encountered. What lessons can you draw from these experiences? How can you apply them to improve your delegation approach going forward?

By openly sharing both your successes and lessons learned, you can create a culture of continuous improvement and inspire others to embrace the power of delegation. After all, becoming a delegation master is a journey, not a destination – and the more you're willing to learn and grow, the more your team and your organization will thrive.

The Long-Term Impact of Successful Delegation

Don't be guilty of throwing Delegation Bombs! Also, don't make the same mistake I did early in my career of delegating with good intentions. We have covered so many techniques, tools, and best practices you can use to design your delegation for success. Consequently, by measuring the success of your delegation efforts, you can ensure that you're constantly improving and maximizing the benefits for everyone involved.

In the next chapter, we'll explore how delegation can be applied in different contexts, from remote teams to high-stakes situations, to help you become a more versatile and effective leader.

CHAPTER 7:
OVERCOMING CHALLENGES, NAVIGATING THE OBSTACLES

• • •

"Delegation requires the willingness to pay for short-term failures in order to gain long-term competency."
— Dave Ramsey

One of the first challenges you have when delegating letting go of "stink'n think'n" as Zig Ziglar used to say. If you find yourself thinking:

"I know I should ask for help, but I don't want to be pushy."
"My team already has enough to do."
"I hate asking people to do things."

Leaders who choose to adhere to these false beliefs keep performance and team engagement low and keep the overall organization from reaching its potential. It sounds harsh, but everyone needs to break free from a little "stink'n think'n" sometimes.

The Boomerang of Death

As we talked about at the start of this chapter, the key to successful delegation is learning the art of letting go. But let's be real: empowering others isn't always easy. One of the toughest challenges you'll run into is what I like to call the **Delegation Boomerang of Death**. Growing up, I was always fascinated by boomerangs. It amazed me how you could throw something away, and it would come right back to you like magic. Delegation can work the same way.

Some leaders hand over tasks but then quickly jump back in at the first sign of a mistake, snatching the work back. Other well-meaning leaders might wait until someone hits a snag and then swoop in to save the day, playing the "fixer" role. As a result, every time there's a hiccup, the team member runs back to the leader for help. In both cases, true delegation never actually happens; the leader just ends up overloaded with work again!

So, don't fall into the trap of being a delegation Re-doer, or you'll find yourself stuck with the Delegation Boomerang of Death. When you delegate something, remember to really give it away!

Here are some common challenges that cause leaders to suffer from the boomerang effect and how to address them:

1. **Fear of losing control**: Remember, effective delegation enhances your control by multiplying your impact. Holding on only lowers your impact and effectiveness.
2. **Perfectionism**: Accept that others might do things differently, but not necessarily worse. Remember the 70% Rule and show grace through the process.
3. **Lack of patience**: View the time invested in delegation as a long-term investment in your team's capabilities.

4. **Resistance from team members**: Some may be uncomfortable with added responsibility. Use the Caveman Method to gradually build their confidence.
5. **Organizational culture**: If your company culture doesn't support empowerment, start small and demonstrate the benefits.

By anticipating and addressing these challenges, you can create an environment where empowering delegation thrives. You can also overcome the pull to take back the work that you recently delegated.

As you continue your delegation journey, remember that empowerment is not just about getting tasks done—it's about developing your team, building a culture of trust and accountability, and ultimately multiplying your impact as a leader. In the words of leadership expert John C. Maxwell, "If you want to do a few small things right, do them yourself. If you want to do great things and make a big impact, learn to delegate."

In the next chapter, we'll explore how to overcome common delegation challenges, ensuring you can navigate any obstacles that arise in your path to becoming a delegation master.

Managing the Risks of Delegation

Delegation isn't without its challenges. What if the task doesn't get done on time, or it doesn't meet your standards? And what if the team member struggles more than you expected? These are all fair points to worry about, but don't let them stop you from delegating altogether. Instead, think ahead and manage the risks.

Leaders often struggle with letting go of control, leading to micromanagement, or conversely, over-delegating without proper oversight, resulting in confusion and mismanagement. These pitfalls often stem from a lack of alignment between individual and organizational goals.

For years, research has shown that one of the central challenges in organizational leadership is **integrating the needs of the individual with the demands of the organization** (Argyris 1964).

> When this integration fails, delegation often becomes a transactional activity, focused solely on task completion rather than personal and professional growth.

For example, if a leader delegates without understanding the team member's motivations, strengths, or developmental needs, they may unintentionally create resentment or disengagement.

To avoid these pitfalls, leaders must adopt a holistic approach to delegation; the process we have covered in this book considers not only the task but also the person to whom it is assigned. This involves asking critical questions:

- Does this task align with the individual's career aspirations or skills?
- Am I providing the resources and support they need to succeed?
- Have I clearly communicated the "why" behind the delegation?

By addressing these considerations, leaders can foster a sense of ownership and alignment that benefits both the individual and the organization. As the research emphasizes, true delegation is about creating an environment where individuals feel their contributions are valued and connected to broader organizational goals.

Remember, occasional failures or setbacks are completely normal when it comes to delegation. In fact, we learn so much more from our mistakes than from things going perfectly. As you work through the Caveman Method, your goal is to create a safe learning environment with checks and balances. This way, if something does go wrong, the entire project doesn't come crashing down. You can coach them through it, they can learn, and then you can all move forward together. The progress method helps you avoid those big disasters that often happen when you just throw a Delegation Bomb out there!

How Do You Handle Mistakes and Failures?

Even if you manage your risks through delegation mistakes are bound to happen. How you handle these moments can make a big difference in the long-term performance and engagement of your team. If your reaction to errors is one of frustration or blame, it can damage trust and discourage your team from taking initiative. However, if you approach mistakes as learning opportunities, you cultivate a growth-oriented culture that encourages resilience and innovation. This sounds intuitive, but the problem is that every leader has areas they lack awareness. As we will see in the following chapters, your Enneagram type might play a role in how you respond to your teams.

For example, I score as a seven-wing eight on the Enneagram assessment. I tend to bring a lot of energy and enthusiasm to a team or an idea. However, that same passion can sometimes come off as aggressive or too direct. Early in my marriage, my wife would often say, "Whoa, why are you so worked up about this? We're just having a conversation!" I'd respond, "Who's worked up? I'm just sharing my thoughts!"

What I eventually realized is that even when I'm completely calm and not feeling any extreme emotion, I can still come across as pretty intense. When I think I'm communicating at about a

5 out of 10 on the passion scale, it's actually landing at an 8 or 9 for my wife. We had some really important discussions about it, and after years of working on it, she learned that my natural passion levels are pretty high and wasn't offended as much. I also learned that especially during serious conversations, I needed to dial it down to a 3 or a 4 on that scale unless I wanted to create unnecessary tension. I was still myself, just more aware of how I was coming across to others.

When an error occurs, as a leader it's not how you respond that is most important. It's how your team members **perceive** your response. As a leader, sometimes we think we respond great, but we actually miss the mark.

> **The best approach is to remain calm and shift the focus to what can be learned from the experience. FOCUS ON THE PROCESS NOT THE PERSON.**

Rather than assigning blame, explore what went wrong and identify ways to prevent similar issues in the future. Most people want to do a good job. By starting with the process you create a space where people are not defensive and can hear coaching and offer constructive feedback.

Analyzing the process or system failure allows you to understand if the mistake stemmed from unclear instructions or a lack of resources. Showing your team member that the mistake doesn't diminish your confidence in them reinforces their trust in your leadership and assures them of your support as they grow. It sounds simple, but showing your team members you care, even through a mistake, builds incredible amounts of trust.

In the words of leadership expert Brené Brown, vulnerability and failure are essential parts of leadership and learning. By handling mistakes with grace and a commitment to learning, you create an environment where your team feels safe to take risks, explore solutions, and continue growing.

Avoiding Over-Delegation and Under-Delegation

Just as it's possible to delegate too little, it's also possible to delegate too much. Over-delegation can leave your team feeling overwhelmed and overburdened, while under-delegation can stifle their development and leave you feeling underutilized.

The key is to find the sweet spot – delegating enough to free up your time and energy, but not so much that you lose touch with the work or your team's capabilities. This is where the Caveman Delegation Method can be particularly helpful. The gradual transition helps keep leaders from throwing too many Delegation Bombs and also gives leaders confidence that they can delegate effectively.

As you navigate this balance, pay attention to the workloads and stress levels of both yourself and your team. Many of our clients use our 1on1's Coaching System as a monthly feedback loop to check in with their team members. You can find out more about our 1on1's Coaching System at www.Perforam.com.

Addressing Common Challenges

Delegating for growth isn't always easy. One common challenge is that not every team member will immediately embrace the opportunity to take on more responsibility. Some may feel intimidated by stretch assignments or unsure of their ability to succeed. In these cases, patience and encouragement go a long way. Never underestimate the number of times you need to tell someone they can do it before they believe you.

Start small. If a team member seems hesitant, give them a manageable challenge first to build their confidence, like the estimation example earlier in the book. We might just begin by giving the person the task of counting equipment. Then, after their confidence is built up, we can transition them to assigning values and estimates and so on. Over time, as they complete these smaller tasks successfully, you can gradually increase the complexity of the assignments. When someone is resistant to change or resistant to stretch goals or delegation, you are battling their beliefs.

It takes time to shift people into a growth mindset where they can see challenges as opportunities for growth rather than potential failures. Start small, and move one step at a time until you win the battle of belief.

It's not always possible to slow-roll the delegation of work. Sometimes delegation comes regardless of how the person on the receiving end feels about the work. Someone quits, dies, or is promoted, and there is an immediate need that must be filled on the team. In these situations, you may not have the luxury of time. However, you can still practice Caveman and even work through the D.O.S. system to help onboard the new team member quickly while still providing support.

In these situations or even in stretch delegation assignments, one challenge can be managing the workload. Your goal is to delegate for the long-term, which means it's important not to overwhelm your team. Ensure that the tasks you delegate are realistic and that the individual has the time and resources necessary to succeed. Delegation should enhance development and create excitement and engagement in the team, not cause burnout.

Delegation is a Journey

Every delegation challenge is an opportunity to learn and improve. By overcoming these common challenges, you'll be able to delegate more effectively and empower your team to take on greater responsibilities. Now, we have covered how you can navigate these obstacles, enhance your delegation skills, and create a more engaged and capable team in the process.

In the next chapter, we'll explore how individual drivers affect delegation efforts, performance, and success. As a leader, you need a tool to better understand yourself, your team, and the interpersonal dynamics you face when you choose to delegate. The Enneagram is a great place to start. If you would like to know your Enneagram type, you can find our Enneagram Assessment at www.Perforam.com.

CHAPTER 8:
TEAM AWARENESS WINS THE DAY

• • •

"Many men go fishing all their lives without knowing it is not fish they are after."
– Henry David Thoreau

If you are going to delegate, your chance of success dramatically increases if you choose the right person to match with the responsibility. We will discuss specific Enneagram types related to delegation in this chapter. However, there are things about a person in addition to the Enneagram that could make a big difference in your task.

> **Leaders who are master delegators know their team!**

Who is a morning person or a night owl?
Who is an extrovert, introvert, or ambivert?
Who is detail-oriented or generalist?
Who has more schedule flexibility, and who is more rigid?
Are they starters, finishers, or doers? (Read Working Genius for more insights.)

What are their strengths and weaknesses?

What are their ambitions, hopes, and dreams? Retirement, opportunity, or something in between?

By learning more about your team, you can increase the chances of success because when you match a person with an activity that resonates, it's like throwing gas on a fire.

Understanding Strengths and Aspirations

Before you can delegate in a way that promotes development, it's essential to understand each team member's strengths, areas for growth, and career aspirations. Without this understanding, delegating a task might miss the mark or even cause frustration if the team member isn't ready or doesn't see the relevance to their future goals.

This starts with regular conversations. Meeting one-on-one with team members to discuss not just their current workload but their long-term career aspirations helps you get a sense of where each person wants to go. Ask open-ended questions: What motivates them? Where do they see themselves in the next few years? What skills do they want to develop? This information becomes the foundation for intentional delegation.

In addition to these discussions, notice how your team members handle their current responsibilities. Are they great at problem-solving? Do they excel in project management? Are they more detail-oriented or more strategic in their approach? These observations help you match the right developmental tasks with the right person.

For instance, if you have a team member who is eager to move into a leadership role, you might delegate small leadership tasks like running a project meeting or coordinating a team effort. This not only gives them experience but also provides you with a way to assess their readiness for larger leadership roles in the future.

For the rest of this chapter and the next two chapters, we will discuss the importance of knowing the personality or drivers of each person on your team. The Enneagram is a great tool for understanding what drives each of your team members.

If you have never taken the Enneagram or are interested in finding out more information about each type, you can visit www.Perforam.com/Enneagram. We even created our own Enneagram assessment, which you can take online.

You might wonder how the Enneagram Types would play out in real life. The following story illustrates the potential issues you can face when delegating.

The Campaign Crunch

At an innovative non-profit organization, Executive Director Ava, a Type Four, was deeply passionate about the organization's mission. Known for her creativity and emotional depth, Ava excelled at connecting with donors and crafting compelling campaigns. However, her tendency to focus on big ideas sometimes left the day-to-day operations in disarray, and her team felt unsure of priorities.

Enter Raj, the Finance Director and a Type Five. Raj thrived on research, analysis, and finding efficient solutions to complex problems. "Ava, your vision is inspiring," Raj said. "But we need a system to turn your ideas into actionable plans without overwhelming the team. Let me create a structure to support your creativity."

Ava reluctantly agreed, handing off detailed planning and financial oversight to Raj. With his analytical skills, Raj developed a data-driven framework that ensured resources were allocated effectively and campaigns stayed on track. His ability to anticipate challenges and provide practical solutions brought clarity to Ava's big-picture thinking.

The partnership became a turning point for the organization. Ava's visionary leadership, combined with Raj's methodical problem-solving, created a harmonious balance that allowed the non-profit to expand its impact significantly. Ava could focus on inspiring stakeholders and dreaming big, while Raj ensured those dreams were grounded in actionable strategies.

The Dance of Compatibility

Delegation is not just a transactional act; it builds relationships. At its core, successful delegation requires aligning interests, communication styles, and strengths. When there's a mismatch—like Ava's visionary creativity occasionally overwhelming the structured pragmatism of someone like Raj—it can lead to missed opportunities and strained relationships.

In this chapter, we'll explore how different Enneagram types approach delegation, both as leaders and team members. Understanding natural pitfalls and compatibility issues can transform delegation into a tool for building stronger, more effective teams. Through this lens, you'll learn how to adjust your delegation approach to match the strengths and challenges of each type.

Using insights from Ava and Raj's story, let's unpack how each Enneagram type navigates delegation pitfalls and compatibility.

Type One
The Reformer

Pitfall: Type Ones can lean toward micromanagement, driven by their pursuit of perfection. They may struggle to trust others to meet their high standards, often taking back delegated tasks to "fix" them.

Compatibility Insight: Type Ones work best with individuals who value structure and precision, such as Types Six and Five. However, they may clash with more spontaneous types, like Sevens or Nines, who thrive on flexibility.

Tip: To delegate effectively, Ones should clearly communicate their expectations upfront but remain open to alternative approaches. Offering constructive feedback rather than rigid criticism helps foster collaboration.

Type Two
The Helper

Pitfall: Twos often overextend themselves and are reluctant to delegate because they fear being seen as less helpful. When they do delegate, they may hover, offering unsolicited assistance.

Compatibility Insight: Twos thrive with team members who value connection, such as Types Four and Nine, but may struggle with more independent types, like Fives or Eights.

Tip: Twos should focus on delegating tasks that align with their team members' strengths and trust them to take ownership. Setting boundaries around their involvement ensures that delegation doesn't turn into micromanagement.

Type Three
The Achiever

Pitfall: Threes often prioritize efficiency and outcomes, which can lead to delegating too quickly without providing sufficient context or support. They may also struggle to relinquish control over high-profile tasks.

Compatibility Insight: Threes align well with driven types like Ones and Sevens but may clash with types that require more time or reflection, such as Fours or Nines.

Tip: Threes should take the time to clarify their vision and provide the resources needed for success. Encouraging team members to take initiative while maintaining a shared sense of purpose enhances compatibility.

Type Four
The Individualist

Pitfall: Fours often hesitate to delegate, fearing their unique vision will be diluted. When they do delegate, they may over-personalize the task, making it difficult for others to contribute.

Compatibility Insight: Fours excel with empathetic types like Twos or Nines but may struggle with highly pragmatic types like Threes or Eights.

Tip: Fours should focus on articulating their vision clearly, allowing space for others to bring complementary strengths to the table. Emphasizing collaboration over ownership can reduce friction.

Type Five
The Investigator

Pitfall: Fives value independence and can resist delegation, feeling it's more efficient to handle tasks themselves. When they do delegate, they may not provide enough context or check in regularly.

Compatibility Insight: Fives work well with analytical types like Ones or Threes but may struggle with more relational types like Twos or Sevens.

Tip: Fives should prioritize clear communication and regular check-ins to ensure alignment. Delegating small tasks first can build trust and confidence in their team's capabilities.

Type Six
The Loyalist

Pitfall: Sixes can struggle with trust, fearing that delegated tasks won't be handled properly. This can lead to over-involvement or hesitation to delegate altogether.

Compatibility Insight: Sixes thrive with reliable types like Ones or Twos but may clash with more autonomous types like Fives or Sevens.

Tip: Sixes should focus on setting clear expectations and creating systems of accountability that build their confidence in the delegation process.

Type Seven
The Enthusiast

Pitfall: Sevens' excitement for new ideas can lead to overcommitting and underdelivering. They may delegate hastily or struggle to follow through on delegated tasks.

Compatibility Insight: Sevens align well with adaptable types like Threes or Nines but may clash with more detail-oriented types like Ones or Fives.

Tip: Sevens should focus on balancing their enthusiasm with discipline, ensuring that delegated tasks are completed with the same energy they were assigned.

Type Eight
The Challenger

Pitfall: Eights' assertive nature can make them overbearing, delegating with an expectation of immediate results but leaving little room for collaboration or creativity.

Compatibility Insight: Eights thrive with confident types like Threes or Sixes but may struggle with more reserved types like Fives or Nines.

Tip: Eights should prioritize empowering their team, balancing their natural drive with patience and support.

Type Nine
The Peacemaker

Pitfall: Nines' desire for harmony can lead to vague delegation, leaving team members unclear about expectations. They may avoid following up to prevent conflict.

Compatibility Insight: Nines work well with understanding types like Twos or Fours but may struggle with more assertive types like Eights or Threes.

Tip: Nines should focus on being clear and assertive in their communication, ensuring that delegation aligns with their team's strengths and goals.

Building Compatibility Through Awareness

As Ava and Raj's story shows, delegation pitfalls often stem from mismatches in personality and expectations. By understanding the unique dynamics of each Enneagram type, you can tailor your delegation strategy to leverage strengths, minimize conflicts, and foster a more cohesive team.

Reflect on your own type and those you work with. What do you typically struggle with as it relates to delegation? ***Do you know your own personal pitfalls?*** How can you adjust your approach to create alignment and empower others? When delegation becomes a dance of compatibility, both leaders and team members thrive.

CHAPTER 9:
HARNESSING YOUR ENNEAGRAM SUPERPOWERS

...

> "Men of genius do not excel in any profession because they labor in it, but they labor in it because they excel."
> **– William Hazlitt**

In the previous chapter, we explored the natural struggles each Enneagram type might face when it comes to delegation. But challenges are only half the story. Each type also brings unique strengths that, when harnessed effectively, can transform delegation from a mere task assignment into a powerful leadership tool.

In this chapter, we'll shift our focus to those strengths—what makes each type a natural at specific aspects of delegation and how you can lean into those strengths to lead more effectively. To begin, let's dive into a story that highlights how understanding and leveraging these strengths can make all the difference.

The Startup Savior

At a fast-growing tech startup, CEO Jonah, a Type Eight, prided himself on being a decisive leader. He saw potential everywhere and wasn't afraid to take risks. However, as the company grew, Jonah began feeling stretched thin. Deadlines slipped through the cracks, and his team seemed hesitant to take initiative.

That's when Maria, the COO and a Type Six, stepped in. "Jonah, you have the vision," she said. "But let's structure it. I'll ensure the team has clear roles and processes, and you can focus on big-picture decisions."

Jonah agreed reluctantly, handing over responsibilities he had clung to. To his surprise, Maria's organizational skills allowed his team to thrive. She anticipated risks, shored up weaknesses, and ensured that Jonah's ideas were translated into actionable plans.

Their collaboration showcased the unique strengths each Enneagram type brings to delegation, highlighting how understanding these strengths can unlock a team's full potential.

Unleashing Delegation Superpowers

Leaders who genuinely want to maximize their team's or organization's potential work diligently to leverage their natural strengths and empower their team members to do the same. Each Enneagram type possesses inherent qualities that, when embraced, can transform the process of delegation from a mundane task into a powerful tool for growth and productivity.

To effectively leverage your team's strengths, leaders should assign tasks that balance challenge and capability. By using Enneagram types as a reference, we can draw on academic research that highlights how task difficulty and perceived importance affect motivation and resource allocation (Ito and Peterson, 1986). Understanding each team member's strengths and motivations enables us to delegate tasks that are appropriately challenging, fostering an environment that promotes engagement and development. When tasks are meaningful, team members feel that their contributions are valued, which supports both personal growth and collective success. On the other hand, if a task is perceived as too difficult or unattainable, motivation tends to decline.

In this chapter, we will explore the unique strengths of each Enneagram type in the context of delegation. By identifying and leveraging these strengths, you can enhance your leadership effectiveness and create a dynamic work environment.

The Strengths of Each Enneagram Type in Delegation

Type One
The Reformer

Strength: Setting high standards and fostering accountability.

Type Ones excel at setting clear expectations and holding their team accountable. Their natural inclination for precision ensures tasks are well-defined and executed to a high standard. Delegation from a One often includes detailed instructions and thoughtful feedback.

How to Leverage This Strength: Use your clarity and structure to create systems for delegation. While you value perfection, focus on coaching your team to achieve excellence rather than micromanaging.

Type Two
The Helper

Strength: Building strong relationships and offering support.

Twos are masters of empathy and connection, making them skilled at building trust within their teams. They naturally encourage and support their team members, fostering a collaborative atmosphere.

How to Leverage This Strength: Use your relational strengths to delegate tasks that align with team members' goals. Be mindful to balance your supportive nature with clear boundaries to avoid over-involvement.

Type Three
The Achiever

Strength: Driving results and inspiring others.

Threes are dynamic leaders who thrive on achieving goals. They have a knack for motivating their team and aligning tasks with the organization's objectives, ensuring progress and results.

How to Leverage This Strength: Delegate with a focus on outcomes, creating a shared vision that inspires your team. Provide regular check-ins to celebrate wins and recalibrate as needed.

Type Four
The Individualist

Strength: Bringing creativity and vision to the process.

Fours bring unique perspectives and creative solutions to delegation. They excel at designing innovative approaches and inspiring others to think outside the box.

How to Leverage This Strength: Delegate tasks that require a creative touch. Share your vision openly and encourage your team to add their own ideas while guiding them toward the desired outcome.

Type Five
The Investigator

Strength: Providing clarity through analysis and insight.

Fives thrive on gathering knowledge and creating thoughtful, data-driven strategies. They excel at breaking down complex tasks into manageable steps, ensuring clarity for their team.

How to Leverage This Strength: Use your analytical skills to delegate tasks with a clear roadmap. Share relevant insights and resources while allowing your team the freedom to explore solutions.

Type Six
The Loyalist

Strength: Creating stability and anticipating challenges.

Sixes are highly attuned to potential risks, making them excellent at planning and contingency management. They build trust through consistency and reliability.

How to Leverage This Strength: Delegate by creating clear structures and backup plans. Use your foresight to identify potential obstacles and provide your team with the tools to overcome them.

Type Seven
The Enthusiast

Strength: Generating excitement and encouraging innovation.

Sevens are energetic leaders who bring positivity and enthusiasm to delegation. They inspire creativity and encourage their teams to think big.

How to Leverage This Strength: Delegate tasks that benefit from brainstorming and innovation. Balance your energy with practical follow-ups to ensure ideas are turned into action.

Type Eight
The Challenger

Strength: Empowering others and driving results.

Eights are natural delegators who instill confidence in their team. They focus on achieving goals and aren't afraid to give others the authority to make decisions.

How to Leverage This Strength: Delegate with confidence, clearly communicating expectations and granting autonomy. Use your assertiveness to support your team and remove obstacles in their way.

Type Nine
The Peacemaker

Strength: Promoting harmony and collaboration.

Nines excel at creating inclusive environments where everyone feels valued. They are natural mediators, fostering cooperation and mutual respect within their teams.

How to Leverage This Strength: Delegate in a way that aligns with your team's strengths and fosters collaboration. Use your calm demeanor to defuse tension and encourage open communication.

Harnessing Your Strengths for Success

Now that you have reviewed all the different types and learned how to harness their strengths, take a minute to reflect on your strengths. Understanding your Enneagram type's strengths can help you refine your delegation approach. Here are three practical ways to harness these strengths:

1. **Reflect on Your Natural Tendencies:** Identify the strengths you already bring to delegation and think about how they've shaped your leadership style. Are you a motivator, a strategist, or a connector?
2. **Leverage Your Strengths Strategically:** Pair your strengths with tasks that align with them. For example, if you're a Type Five, focus on delegating tasks that require analysis and precision.
3. **Complement Your Strengths:** Recognize areas where you might need support and delegate to team members whose strengths complement your own. For instance, if you're a Type Four struggling with structure, seek out a Type One team member to balance your delegation.

Building a Strengths-Based Delegation Culture

As Jonah and Maria's story demonstrates, delegation success often lies in understanding and leveraging each person's unique strengths. By embracing your Enneagram type's superpowers, you can delegate with confidence, empowering your team and driving meaningful results.

Reflect on your delegation practices and ask yourself: How can I use my strengths to elevate my team? What are the strengths of each of my team members? What seems to drive each person? When you align your natural gifts with the needs of your organization, you create a culture where everyone's talents are valued, and your team thrives.

CHAPTER 10:
TAILORING COMMUNICATION AND MOTIVATION

...

"A man will fight harder for his interests than for his rights."
– Napoleon Bonaparte

Delegating tasks is one thing, but delegating work to someone who is excited about the challenge is rocket fuel! Is it possible to motivate the team to deliver their best work? Yes! Communication and motivation are at the heart of successful delegation, and the Enneagram offers a powerful framework to understand how different personalities prefer to give and receive instructions.

In this chapter, we'll explore two critical dimensions of delegation:

1. **Communication Styles by Enneagram Type** – How to tailor your approach to ensure clarity and connection.
2. **Motivating Each Enneagram Type Through Delegation** – How to align tasks with the unique drivers of each type to inspire engagement.

Let's start with a case study to illustrate how communication and motivation can transform delegation outcomes.

Bridging the Gap Between Styles

David, a Type Eight manager, prides himself on his direct, no-nonsense leadership style. He thrives on autonomy and expects his team to embrace the same independence. When delegating to Rachel, a Type Six team member, he handed her a high-stakes project with minimal instructions, saying, "You've got this—let me know if you hit a wall."

Rachel, on the other hand, found David's approach overwhelming. Without clear guidelines or regular check-ins, she felt insecure about the project's direction and struggled to move forward. Misaligned communication and motivation left both frustrated—David felt Rachel wasn't stepping up, and Rachel felt unsupported.

However, David and Rachel took the Enneagram assessment. They learned about each other's types and communication preferences. By understanding their Enneagram types, David learned to provide Rachel with the structure and reassurance she needed, while Rachel grew more confident in asking for clarity. This shift not only improved the project's outcome but also strengthened their working relationship.

The Key to Delegation Compatibility

Each Enneagram type approaches work, communication, and responsibility differently, and these differences can either enhance or hinder collaboration. Tailoring your communication style to each team member is essential for successful delegation. Data supports the idea that people respond to delegation differently, influenced by factors like gender, personality, and individual preferences (Akinola, Martin, and Phillips 2018). **This means what works for one person might not work for another.** For example, some team members may need detailed instructions and reassurance, while others may prefer a more hands-off approach that allows for greater independence. A transformational leader will apply the Caveman Delegation Method in slightly different ways to suit the needs of individual team members.

By understanding these unique preferences and adapting how you communicate and delegate, you build stronger trust and alignment within your team. This personalized approach not only improves collaboration but also creates a more supportive and effective work environment where everyone can thrive.

In this chapter, we'll explore the unique dynamics of delegating to each type and how compatibility between delegator and delegatee can make or break your delegation efforts. Whether you're assigning tasks, processes, or outcomes, understanding what drives each type can help you connect on a deeper level and create meaningful results.

Let's begin by examining how delegation styles can complement—or conflict with—individual types.

Delegation Compatibility by Enneagram Type

Type	Preferred Style	Delegating To Them
Type 1	Detailed and structured. Appreciates precise instructions and clear expectations.	Provide a checklist or framework and clarify quality standards and timelines upfront.
Type 2	Personal and affirming. Values connection and recognition in communication.	Frame tasks as opportunities to help others. Use encouraging language to reinforce their unique contributions.
Type 3	Concise and results-focused. Appreciates efficiency and goal-oriented communication.	Highlight how the task aligns with broader objectives. Keep discussions brief and outcome-focused.
Type 4	Thoughtful and creative. Values space for self-expression and originality.	Encourage creative input and provide flexibility. Avoid overly rigid instructions.

Type 5	Clear and logical. Prefers detailed, factual information without unnecessary embellishment.	Provide relevant data and context upfront. Allow for independence while remaining available for questions.
Type 6	Reassuring and collaborative. Needs clarity and guidance to feel secure.	Offer a clear roadmap and regular check-ins. Reassure them of their capabilities and support.
Type 7	Energetic and optimistic. Thrives on engaging, dynamic communication.	Focus on exciting aspects of the task. Allow flexibility in their approach.
Type 8	Direct and straightforward. Values autonomy and clear, no-nonsense communication.	Be upfront about expectations and give authority over the task. Avoid micromanagement.
Type 9	Inclusive and encouraging. Responds well to collaborative, non-confrontational communication.	Provide gentle encouragement to take ownership. Clarify priorities to reduce potential indecision.

Motivating Each Enneagram Type Through Delegation

Type	Core Motivation	How to Motivate
Type 1	A desire to improve and do things right.	Assign tasks where their attention to detail can shine. Frame assignments as opportunities to make a positive impact.
Type 2	A need to feel valued and connected.	Highlight how the task benefits others. Recognize their contributions and emphasize their importance to the team.
Type 3	A drive for success and recognition.	Delegate high-visibility tasks with clear performance metrics. Recognize accomplishments publicly.
Type 4	A longing for authenticity and creativity.	Assign projects that allow personal expression or innovation. Affirm their unique perspective.

Type 5	A need for knowledge and autonomy.	Offer tasks that require problem-solving or specialized expertise. Respect their independence.
Type 6	A desire for security and support.	Emphasize stability and importance. Reassure them and provide consistent guidance.
Type 7	A craving for excitement and variety.	Delegate dynamic tasks. Highlight the fun aspects and allow room for creativity.
Type 8	A need for control and impact.	Assign leadership roles or high-stakes responsibilities. Provide autonomy and respect their authority.
Type 9	A longing for harmony and inclusion.	Delegate collaborative tasks. Encourage their input and affirm their contributions to create a sense of belonging.

Connecting Communication and Motivation

As we have discussed at length in this book, delegation is both an art and a science. By aligning your communication style with the preferences of each Enneagram type and leveraging their core motivations, you can increase the motivation of the team and unlock their full potential.

When done thoughtfully, delegation becomes a tool not just for efficiency but for growth, trust, and mutual success. Use these insights to create a work environment where every team member feels seen, understood, and empowered to thrive.

In the next chapter, it's time to take a breath and end where we started. We will review how the concepts and tools in this book help pull you out of the ants and keep you focused on the elephants in your organization and create a strong legacy of leadership.

CHAPTER 11:
LEADERSHIP DEVELOPMENT AND LEGACY

...

> "When you delegate tasks, you create followers. When you delegate authority, you create leaders."
> **- Craig Groeschel**

Keith and Chris's Story

Keith knew his time in his role as a manager was limited. He had been told he was being promoted in one year to oversee half the company's operations—a massive opportunity, but one that left a glaring challenge in its wake. No one was prepared to step into Keith's shoes. Without a ready successor, Keith worried about the long-term stability of his team.

There was, however, one possibility: Chris. Bright, capable, and values-driven, Chris showed immense promise, but he was young—by far the youngest candidate for a managerial role in the company's history. Keith saw potential in Chris, even when Chris doubted himself.

After breaking the news to Chris, Keith faced an uphill battle. Chris was overwhelmed, voicing concerns about his lack of leadership experience and readiness for the role. But Keith wasn't deterred. Instead, he laid out a clear path. Using the company's 1-on-1 Coaching System and applying Caveman Delegation principles, Keith developed a timeline of gradual responsibilities Chris would take on, month by month, to prepare him for leadership.

Chris started small, leading safety meetings and learning other important tasks. Gradually, he shadowed Keith in client meetings and took charge of maintaining key client relationships. By the end of the year, Chris had not only mastered the position but also introduced innovative ideas that strengthened the team. When Keith stepped into his new role, Chris stepped into his, confident and capable, exceeding all expectations.

This story is more than just a success story; it's a blueprint for how intentional delegation can create future leaders. In this chapter, we'll explore how delegation is not only a tool for task management but also a vehicle for leadership development and building a legacy.

Delegation as a Leadership Growth Tool

When leaders focus on growing their team members through delegation, they simultaneously sharpen their own leadership skills. It requires patience, vision, and the ability to recognize potential in others, even when they don't see it in themselves. Let's look at how Keith managed to delegate to his future replacement so successfully.

Lessons from Keith's Approach:

1. **Clarity in Vision**

    Keith didn't just tell Chris about the promotion—he painted a clear picture of what the journey would look like. He laid out specific milestones and ensured Chris understood the long-term goals.

2. **Gradual Responsibility Building**

    Rather than overwhelming Chris, Keith broke the role into manageable pieces, delegating responsibilities step by step. This gradual approach gave Chris time to grow and succeed in each area before adding more.

3. **Accountability and Feedback**

   Monthly 1-on-1 sessions ensured Chris had regular feedback and guidance. Keith didn't just hand off tasks; he stayed connected, offering support and celebrating wins along the way.

4. **Trust and Autonomy**

   Keith trusted Chris to rise to the occasion and gave him room to make decisions. This trust empowered Chris to take ownership and even innovate within the role.

Building a Leadership Pipeline

> Leaders who focus on developing others create a ripple effect, ensuring their teams can thrive long after they've moved on.

Keith's story is actually not fictional; it's a real example (although the names have been changed). Chris really did step into the new role, and after 3 years in the position, he is doing better than ever. Keith even says that Chris is better than he was!

A strong leadership pipeline ensures continuity and growth within an organization. Research (Galbraith 1973) emphasizes the importance of structuring organizations to facilitate role clarity and growth. By strategically delegating responsibilities that align with leadership development goals, leaders can create a pipeline of future talent. When leaders delegate strategically, they:

- Identify and nurture high-potential individuals.
- Reduce the risk of burnout by spreading leadership responsibilities.
- Create a culture of learning and development.

How to Build a Leadership Pipeline

So now that you have all the tools, it's time to take the next step and use delegation to build your leadership pipeline. Let's study what great leaders do to grow their pipeline:

1. **Identify Potential Leaders:** Look for team members with the skills, values, and attitudes aligned with leadership. Potential isn't always obvious—sometimes it requires vision to see what others can't.
2. **Start with Small Wins:** Give emerging leaders tasks or projects that build confidence and demonstrate their capabilities.
3. **Delegate Process-Level Responsibilities:** As discussed in earlier chapters, delegating processes rather than tasks gives team members opportunities to develop management skills.
4. **Stretch Assignments:** Challenge team members with projects slightly beyond their current comfort zone to accelerate growth.
5. **Mentorship Through Delegation:** Use delegation as a mentorship tool. Provide context, guidance, and feedback to help team members learn and grow.

Creating a Legacy Through Delegation

True leadership isn't about handling every little thing by yourself; it's about fostering an environment where others can thrive. Delegation is key in building a lasting impact. Think about your favorite coach, teacher, or boss for a moment. When their name pops into your mind, you probably feel a mix of gratitude and respect. It's not because they showered you with money; it's because they recognized potential in you that you might not have even noticed. They took the time to coach, guide, teach, and encourage you in ways that transformed how you see the world, made you a better person, and opened up new opportunities for you.

> Delegation isn't a transaction; it's an investment in trust, growth, and the future.

What Does a Delegation Legacy Look Like?
- **Empowered Teams:** Teams that can operate effectively without constant supervision. They have the tools, resources, authority, autonomy, and motivation to be successful.
- **Sustainable Growth:** How long could your team or organization run without you showing up at the office? A day? A week? A month? A year? Your legacy is being so good at delegation that the entire organization or team would thrive even in your absence.
- **Elevated Standards:** We talked earlier about delegation KPIs. The standards you set and maintain are part of the legacy you leave. A culture where excellence and innovation are the norms is one that is full of amazing delegators!

Consider these questions:
- Who are you preparing to take your place?
- Are you empowering your team to make decisions and lead?
- How will your organization look when you're no longer in your current role?

> Delegation isn't just about the tasks you hand off today—it's about the **leaders you cultivate** for tomorrow.

The Chris Effect

Keith's intentional approach to delegation didn't just prepare Chris for a new role; it transformed the entire team. Chris's innovations, confidence, and leadership set a new standard, proving that delegation is one of the most powerful tools a leader has.

As you reflect on your own delegation journey, ask yourself: What kind of legacy do you want to leave? Are you using delegation to empower and elevate those around you? The leaders you develop today will shape the future of your organization—and that's a legacy worth investing in.

CHAPTER 12:
THE HEART OF LEADERSHIP

• • •

"If you aren't going all the way, why go at all?"
— **Joe Namath**

Remember how we started this journey? With a story about a curse—the curse of capability. That overwhelming feeling of "I can, so I should" that leaves so many talented leaders exhausted, stretched thin, and unable to reach their full potential. Now, as we conclude our exploration of delegation, it's time to break free from that curse once and for all.

Throughout this book, we've discovered that delegation isn't just about managing tasks—it's about transforming leadership itself.

> Every task delegated is a step toward multiplying your leadership potential.

We've learned that being capable doesn't mean we should do everything ourselves. Instead, our capabilities should be focused on elevating others, building strong teams, and creating lasting impact. Let's revisit the core principles that can transform you from a capable but overwhelmed leader to a masterful delegator who builds legacy through others:

The Foundation:

To understand our "Why," we began by exploring the fundamental truth that delegation isn't about offloading work—it's about maximizing impact. Just as we discussed the elephants (big initiatives) and ants (small tasks) in organizations, effective delegation helps you stay focused on what truly matters while empowering others to grow without getting overwhelmed by all the ants. Let's review some of the practical tools in your new delegation toolbelt that make delegation both systematic and successful:

- The Responsibility Levels: Understanding task, process, and outcome delegation
- The Delegation Matrix: Helping you identify what to delegate
- The Caveman Method: Providing a simple, memorable approach to transfer responsibilities
- The D.O.S. Framework: Ensuring alignment between dangers, opportunities, and strengths

The Human Element:

Understanding people lies at the heart of successful delegation. When we delegate tasks, processes, or outcomes, we're not just assigning work - we're engaging with individuals who bring their own perspectives, motivations, and ways of working. Through the Enneagram, we've gained profound insights into how different personalities approach work and respond to delegation. This understanding helps us recognize that successful delegation requires more than just processes - it demands empathy, clear communication, and alignment with each team member's natural strengths.

Consider how different personalities engage with work: Some thrive on detailed instructions while others prefer creative freedom. Some are motivated by public recognition, while others find satisfaction in quiet achievement. By understanding these differences through tools like the Enneagram, we can match tasks with natural strengths and create opportunities that resonate with each individual's motivations.

This human element extends beyond just matching tasks to strengths. It's about creating an environment where team members feel empowered to grow, take risks, and develop new capabilities. When we understand what drives each person, we can provide the right balance of support and autonomy, ensuring they feel confident and capable in their delegated responsibilities.

From Theory to Practice:

The journey from understanding delegation principles to implementing them effectively requires a transformation in how we think about leadership and team development. As we move from theory to practice, we see how delegation becomes a powerful tool for both individual growth and organizational success.

When leaders embrace effective delegation, they witness remarkable changes. When leaders align delegation with both personal and organizational values, they create an environment of trust and purpose (Ren, 2010). Teams become more engaged and proactive, taking ownership of their work with pride and purpose. Individual team members develop new skills and confidence, stepping up to challenges they might have previously avoided. The organization becomes more agile and responsive, with multiple capable hands ready to tackle emerging opportunities and challenges.

This transformation doesn't happen overnight - it's a gradual process that requires patience, consistency, and commitment. Leaders must be willing to invest time upfront, knowing that the long-term benefits far outweigh the initial investment. They need to trust the process, even when it feels uncomfortable or slower than doing things themselves.

The Legacy Factor:
Perhaps the most profound impact of masterful delegation lies in its ability to create a lasting legacy. When leaders delegate effectively, they don't just accomplish tasks - they build future leaders who can carry the organization forward. This multiplier effect transforms individual capability into organizational strength.

The legacy of effective delegation extends far beyond immediate task completion. It creates a culture of trust and empowerment where innovation thrives. Team members develop confidence in their abilities and feel invested in the organization's success. They begin to think strategically, take initiative, and develop their own leadership capabilities.

This ripple effect continues long after the original leader has moved on. The skills, mindsets, and culture they've cultivated through thoughtful delegation become part of the organization's DNA. Future generations of leaders emerge, ready to face new challenges with confidence and competence. In this way, delegation becomes more than a management technique - it becomes a catalyst for creating enduring impact and sustainable success.

By focusing on these human elements, implementing practical strategies, and building lasting legacy, leaders can transform their organizations through the power of effective delegation. The impact extends far beyond task completion, creating a culture of growth, innovation, and sustained excellence that benefits everyone involved.

Your Call to Action:

Now it's your turn. The knowledge you've gained through this book is powerful, but only if you put it into practice. Here are your next steps:

1. **Start Small but Start Now**
    - Review your current tasks using the Delegation Matrix
    - Identify one responsibility you can delegate this week
    - Create a delegation strategy using the tools provided
2. **Build Your System**
    - Apply the Caveman Method to ensure a successful transfer
    - Set clear KPIs for measuring delegation success
    - Establish regular check-ins to monitor progress
3. **Invest in People**
    - Use the Enneagram insights to understand your team better
    - Match tasks with individual strengths and aspirations
    - Focus on developing future leaders through intentional delegation
4. **Monitor and Adjust**
    - Regularly assess your delegation effectiveness
    - Celebrate successes and learn from challenges
    - Continue refining your approach

Breaking the Curse:

Remember that lawn mower story from the beginning? That moment of revelation about the need to delegate better? Since that time, I have worked hard to restructure many aspects of my life. I am more productive now than ever. Don't fall into the same trap! You're equipped with everything you need to avoid that trap of capability and create something far more powerful—**a legacy of leadership that multiplies impact through others**. The journey from capable individual to masterful delegator isn't always easy, but it's always worth it. As you implement these principles, you'll find yourself:

- Less overwhelmed and more strategic
- Leading with greater impact
- Building stronger teams
- Creating lasting value

> Delegation isn't just a skill—it's a transformation. It's the difference between being a capable individual and being a transformational leader.

It's the key to breaking free from the curse of capability and stepping into your full potential as a leader.

Your journey to masterful delegation starts now. Maybe you need to take a few rides on your lawn mower and think it over! Take what you've learned, put it into practice, and watch as your leadership impact multiplies through the people you empower. The curse of capability ends here, replaced by the power of intentional delegation and the promise of a lasting legacy.

> Your greatest contribution as a leader isn't what you can do yourself—it's what you can inspire, enable, and empower others to achieve.

Now, it's time to take action and delegate with purpose, passion, and vision. Your team, your organization, and your legacy are waiting.

BIBLIOGRAPHY BY CHAPTER

...

Introduction

1. "Eaten Alive By Ants." History Snoop, 13 Mar 2024, https://www.historysnoop.com/eaten-alive-by-ants/.

Chapter 1: The Importance of Delegation

2. Leana, C. R. (1986). Predictors and consequences of delegation. Academy of Management Journal, 29(4), 754-774.
3. Maxwell, J. C. (2022). The 21 Irrefutable Laws of Leadership: Follow Them and People Will Follow You (25th Anniversary Edition). HarperCollins Leadership. ISBN: 9781400236169.
4. Harvard Business Review. "Delegation Saves Leaders 20% of Their Time." Harvard Business Review, 2016.
5. Schriesheim, C. A., Neider, L. L., & Scandura, T. A. (1998). Delegation and Leader-Member Exchange.
6. American Psychological Association. (2018). *2018 Work and Well-Being Survey*. https://www.apa.org/news/press/releases/stress/2018/work-stress
7. Badal, S. B., & Ott, B. (2015, April 14). Delegating: A Huge Management Challenge for Entrepreneurs. Gallup Business Journal. Retrieved from https://news.gallup.com/

businessjournal/182414/delegating-huge-management-challenge-entrepreneurs.aspx
8. Burnett, Dallas. (2024). *MOVE!: From where you are to where you want to be*. Thrive Publishing LLC.

Chapter 2: Recognizing the Right Moments to Delegate

9. Yukl, G., & Fu, P. P. (1999). Determinants of Delegation and Consultation by Managers.
10. Blanchard, K., & Johnson, S. (1982). *The one minute manager*. New York: William Morrow and Company.
11. Sullivan, Dan. *Unique Ability: Creating the Life You Want*. Strategic Coach, 2001.
12. Schleckser, J. (2016). *Great CEOs are lazy: How exceptional CEOs do more in less time*. Washington, DC: Inc. Original.
13. Covey, Stephen R. *The 7 Habits of Highly Effective People*. Simon & Schuster, 1989.
14. Training Industry. (n.d.). *How a man who didn't think he was up to the job helped put man on the moon*. Retrieved from https://trainingindustry.com/articles/leadership/how-a-man-who-didnt-think-he-was-up-to-the-job-helped-put-man-on-the-moon/

Chapter 3: What to Delegate

15. Wiseman, Liz. *Multipliers: How the Best Leaders Make Everyone Smarter*. Harper Business, 2010.
16. Covey, Stephen R. *The 7 Habits of Highly Effective People*. Simon & Schuster, 1989.
17. The Connection Between Employee Trust and Financial Performance. Harvard Business Review, July 2016. Accessed November 20, 2024. https://hbr.org/2016/07/the-connection-between-employee-trust-and-financial-performance.

18. Collins, J. (2001). *Good to great: Why some companies make the leap...and others don't*. Harper Business.
19. Johnstone, A. (2000). *The Impact of Delegation on Employee Motivation and Performance.*

Chapter 4: Choosing the Right Person

20. DeSimone, R. (2019, December 12). *Improve work performance with a focus on employee development*. Gallup. https://www.gallup.com/workplace/269405/high-performance-workplaces-differently.aspx
21. Hersey, Paul, and Blanchard, Ken. *Management of Organizational Behavior: Utilizing Human Resources*. Pearson, 1982.
22. Hersey, P., & Blanchard, K. H. (1970s). *Skill Will Matrix*. Retrieved from https://situational.com/blog/the-four-leadership-styles-of-situational-leadership/
23. Rezvani, S. (2019, February 27). *Why companies should give women more stretch assignments*. Association for Talent Development. https://www.td.org/content/atd-blog/why-companies-should-give-women-more-stretch-assignments
24. China Europe International Business School (CEIBS). (n.d.). *Jack Welch's Work-Out Program: A Revolution in Leadership*. Retrieved from https://www.ceibs.edu/new-papers-columns/22566
25. Schriesheim, C. A., Neider, L. L., & Scandura, T. A. (1998). *Delegation and Leader-Member Exchange.*

Chapter 5: The Caveman Delegation Method

26. Bandura, Albert. "Social Learning Theory." *Psychological Review*, vol. 84, no. 2, 1977, pp. 191-215.
27. Vygotsky, Lev S. *Mind in Society: The Development of Higher Psychological Processes*. Harvard University Press, 1978.

28. Explain Everything. (n.d.). *How to Master the "I Do, We Do, You Do" Model Approach to Teaching.* Retrieved from https://explaineverything.com/blog/inspiring-educators/how-to-master-the-i-do-we-do-you-do-model-approach-to-teaching.
29. Graen, G. B., & Uhl-Bien, M. (1995). *Leader-Member Exchange Theory.*

Chapter 6: Designing Delegation for Success
30. Drescher, G. (2017). *Delegation Outcomes: Perceptions of Leaders and Followers.*
31. Sullivan, Dan. *The Strategic Coach Approach to Delegation.* Strategic Coach, 2003.

Chapter 7: Overcoming Common Delegation Challenges
32. Argyris, C. (1964). *Integrating the Individual and the Organization.*

Chapter 9: Harnessing Your Enneagram Superpowers
33. Ito, J. K., & Peterson, R. S. (1986). *Effects of Task Difficulty and Importance on Helping and Reward Allocation Behaviors.*

Chapter 10: Delegation Communication Styles
34. Akinola, M., Martin, A., & Phillips, K. (2018). *To Delegate or Not to Delegate: Gender Differences in Affective Associations and Behavioral Responses to Delegation.*

Chapter 11: Mentoring Through Delegation
35. Galbraith, J. R. (1973). *Designing Complex Organizations.*

Chapter 12: Conclusion

36. Ren, T. (2010). *Value Congruence as a Source of Intrinsic Motivation.*
37. Sinek, Simon. *Start With Why: How Great Leaders Inspire Everyone to Take Action.* Penguin, 2009.
38. Covey, Stephen R. *The 7 Habits of Highly Effective People.* Simon & Schuster, 1989.

ACKNOWLEDGMENTS

...

First, I would like to thank my wife, Danielle, who has supported me for more than 20 years. For the past three books, she has drawn the short straw, reading numerous versions of each manuscript before giving me the final thumbs up. She has always been my biggest fan and is still my best friend.

To my parents, to whom this book is dedicated, thank you for prioritizing teaching my brothers and me the 'why' behind what we do, rather than just the 'what.' How we apply information may change, but principles are timeless and provide clarity when we need it most. I truly appreciate your guidance.

I would also like to thank all the team members I have had the privilege to lead and serve throughout my career. Thank you for walking with me as we developed many of these concepts together. I appreciate your openness when I rushed into your office (or cubicle) with a crazy idea that needed your expertise. Without you, the success of our projects and the writing of this book would not have been possible. I have always valued your contributions and cherished your friendship.

Finally, thank you to everyone who played a role in bringing this book to life, from editing to typesetting to cover layout and design. It is an honor to work with such a talented group of individuals. Thank you for allowing me to "delegate" the work that you excelled at much more than I ever could!

RESOURCES

...

We are so thankful you purchased and enjoyed Caveman Delegation. We would love to connect with you. Join our performance management community at www.Perforam.com/Community.

Also please consider reading other books written by Dallas Burnett, including:

- **LIFT** – A business fable for teams and the people who lead them
- **MOVE!** – From where you are to where you want to be

Perforam is a Performance Management Company. We specialize in helping companies increase employee performance.

Check out www.Perforam.com to learn more about:

1on1's Coaching System: Are you looking to increase coaching and development on your team or organization? Try our new 1on1's Coaching System App. Learn more about it at www.ThinkMoveThrive.com/1on1-app/

5 | 25 Reviews – Everyone hates performance reviews. Isn't it time you tried something different? Our 5 | 25 Reviews are not the same old "ratings for raises," we take a different approach. Our reviews focus on increasing engagement and performance!

Assessments – Join our community so you can get access to our unique Enneagram Assessment (built for leaders and business teams) and ALIGN, the assessment helping businesses understand culture and employee engagement in new ways that help drive performance.

www.ingramcontent.com/pod-product-compliance
Lightning Source LLC
LaVergne TN
LVHW090116080426
835507LV00040B/916